MIND LEAP

MIND LEAP

THE KEY TO UNLOCKING
THE MIND'S POTENTIAL

JONATHON CRAMER

NEW DEGREE PRESS

MIND LEAP

The Key to Unlocking the Mind's Potential

ISBN

978-1-64137-338-8   *Paperback*

978-1-64137-656-3   *Ebook*

CONTENTS

INTRODUCTION

———

Artificial intelligence (A.I) is moving fast. So fast, that if humans want to stay relevant in a future dominated by artificial intelligence, they must become cyborgs, warns Elon Musk. Musk argues that as A.I. "becomes more sophisticated, there will be fewer and fewer jobs that a robot can't do better".[1]

Wait a second.

This sounds a lot like the premonitions imposed by the hit 1999 film, *The Matrix*.

However, in *The Matrix*, humans were still employed. They weren't irrelevant. Robots in the film used the electronic currents in the human body to assemble a grid-like array of biological human batteries. In doing so, they would have access to a sustainable source of energy for their foreseeable future.

But a bit of a misalignment still exists between fiction and reality. It assumes that robots, in collaboration with A.I., can achieve a sentient status, a mode of thinking enriched by feeling and emotion, and with it, a sense of animosity toward humanity. I don't buy this idea. Humans have yet to even come close to understanding the neurological basis for our emotions let alone installing some type of behavioral-mandating software into a robot.

In other words, we should worry less about A.I. suddenly disobeying orders and enacting a route to enslave us, but more about A.I. being hyper-obedient, following orders without question or restraint. For large corporations filled with software developers, it's all too easy to see where things can go wrong. As the digital revolution of the twenty-first century gains more momentum than ever before, with just a few algorithms, computer programmers will have the power to alter the very fabric of both the social and environmental hierarchy of life as we know it.

But before you throw this book down and start calling all your software developer friends asking them to spare your life, it's important to note that even though technology can be used dangerously, the technology itself is never **deterministic**.

"Every technology opens different doors to different social and political systems. In the twentieth century, we could use the technology of the industrial revolution: electricity, trains, radio, and television, to build communistic dictatorships or fascist regimes or liberal democracies. The electricity didn't tell you what to do with it. It's the same with A.I." [2]

In other words, it's up to us, not the A.I., to make the final decisions about how technology ought to be used. Still, this idea is just scratching the surface.

The reason many big thinkers like Harari are so alarmed by A.I. is not necessarily because of the lines of code programming it, but because it has the potential to reprogram us. How sure are you that the last purchase you made on Amazon or the last movie recommended to you on Netflix wasn't influenced by A.I.? Memorizing maps has become a thing of the past with Google's near-instant GPS navigation, and finding out who to date has never been easier with modern dating apps like Bumble and Tinder. And as A.I. grows and more companies employ its use, much of the mundane tasks necessary to support basic survival needs will become obsolete. However, when presented with these facts, the human-animal starts to go on the defensive. A proud animal likes to affirm his role and place in the world by the decisions it makes. When you take that element away, what's left may just be the very scaffolding that supports its defining personality traits. And if it leaves its sense of self unchanged, chances are A.I. will not only start automating its decisions but will also start constructing a more updated version of who it thinks it is. In effect, the human-animal will be hacked by A.I. without even knowing it.

As proud Homo sapiens, we must realize that A.I. presents us with an interesting ultimatum. If abused, A.I. has the potential to be very dangerous depending on who's in control of it, as Harari points out.

On the other hand, it gives us an exciting opportunity to shed ourselves from the mundane tasks of everyday life. As it sweeps through the millions of acres of crops, revolutionizes financial paperwork, and constructs ultra-efficient manu-facturing facilities, A.I. will surely automate a whole host of jobs as Musk stated. But, funny enough, this book is not about the cyborg revolution or some innovative way to use A.I. and personalize health care or education.

No. This book is about a completely different technology, which doesn't require surgery or extensive knowledge of computer science.

*This book is about psychedelics and how they can serve as **trans-formative tools** to collectively extend both the cognitive and emotional capacities of the human mind so we can become more conscious of the incoming dangers that technology and our world present in the twenty-first century. There's a lot more to* *psychedelics than meets the eye, and often, we forget how they have played and can play a major role in the evolution of humanity.*

SAVING EDUCATION WITH PSYCHEDELICS

At the forefront of human evolution, we usually think of education as its primary catalyst. After all, the educational facilities of the world nourish the future generations of our species, right?

The problem with modern education is that much of what constitutes quality education in many regions of the world is just rudimentary memorization. Or what has now become a taboo phrase in schools, **rote-learning**.

With standardized tests standing at the pinnacle of modern education, many schools have become less focused on giving kids a quality education. Instead, they resort to tactics designed to increase their students' SAT/ACT scores. As James Popham, a UCLA graduate school professor, argues, "These days, if a school's standardized test scores are high, people think the school's staff is effective. If a school's standardized test scores are low, they see the school's staff as ineffective. In either case, because *educational quality is being measured by the wrong yardstick*, those evaluations are apt to be in error."

In many schools, bringing a formula sheet into a test is tantamount to heresy. Let's be honest—as A.I. starts optimizing many mathematical fundamentals and auto-populates our devices with rich diction, memorizing a formula or vocabulary list becomes less than useless.

Ben Orlin, a high school teacher in Oakland, states, "Memorization is a frontage road: It runs parallel to the best parts of learning, never intersecting. It's a detour around all the action, a way of *knowing without learning, of answering without understanding*." [3]

In 2018, The World Bank wrote and published an entire report called "LEARNING to Realize Education's Promise", which details the worldwide *learning crisis*. Here are a few notable quotes:

- "In rural India, just under three-quarters of students in grade 3 could not solve a two-digit subtraction such as 46 – 17, and by grade 5 half could still not do so."

- "Some teachers have been found to concentrate on test-specific skills instead of untested subjects, and some schools have engaged in strategic behavior to ensure that only the better-performing students are tested, such as assigning students to special education that excuses them from testing."

- "Rabia Nura, a sixteen-year-old girl from Kano in northern Nigeria, goes to school despite ever-present threats from Boko Haram. She is determined to become a doctor (Smith 2014). But 37 million African children will learn so little in school that they will not be much better off than kids who never attend school".[4]

Sir Ken Robinson supplements this *learning crisis* perspective in his 2013 TED Talk, *How to Escape Education's Death Valley*, announcing, "In place of curiosity, what we have is a culture of compliance. Our children and teachers are encouraged to follow routine algorithms rather than to excite that power of imagination and curiosity."

Among many of these alarming observations, something is clearly wrong with how we are conceptualizing education. In his talk, Robinson furthers the idea of an *education revolution*, pointing out that, "If there's no learning going on, there's no education going on. And people can spend an awful lot of time discussing education without ever discussing learning. The whole point of education is to get people to learn."[5]

For the last two years, I've tutored hundreds of students at The University of Texas at Austin in classes like organic chemistry and differential calculus. I've found that these ill-received perceptions of education have only been further instilled into my mind. Students often come to me with pages filled with notes detailing the exact route to do a specific problem. When I give them a problem, similar in nature, they start flipping through their notes and realize they never actually learned anything at all. They just wrote down how to do one specific problem. It's rather obvious why a student finds courses like organic chemistry irrelevant. They're not learning anything and, instead, have resorted to rote learning as a tactic to make good grades and forget all the value presented within these core classes.

Naturally, I gravitated away from trying to fix education from the top down by teaching students alternative methods to solve problems. Without a fundamental understanding of the subject material, adding another route just adds more complexity to their learning experience.

In order to revolutionize our mental capacities and collect broader understandings about our nature, I realized it's important we take a bottom-up approach by investigating exactly how the mind receives information. However, to understand one's sense of self, how they learn best, what their passions are and where they see themselves in just five years is no easy task. The problem is that, by design, the human mind is not built for the twenty-first century. Exponential technologies like A.I. will only learn faster, and as automation starts to sweep through the job market, the jobs that exist presently will begin fading away. 'More now than ever before, we need a tool that allows us to broaden our perspective about the world and our role in it before the silent doomsday of A.I. reaches completion.

PSYCHEDELIC CEOS

Enter psychedelics, a class of drugs once used by early hominids, abused and stigmatized in the late twentieth century, and now making a comeback in the twenty-first century. Before we visit the main concepts in this book, I think it's important to get a few of our definitions straight.

Drug – A chemical substance used in the treatment, cure, prevention, or diagnosis of disease or used to otherwise *enhance physical or mental well-being.*

Tool – A device or implement, especially one held in the hand, used to carry out a *particular function.*

Interestingly, the modern drug/health market seems to have lost sight of these definitions. "Of the nearly $30 billion that health companies now spend on medical marketing each year, around 68 percent (or about $20 billion) goes to persuading doctors and other medical professionals—not consumers—of the benefits of prescription drugs".[6]

Doesn't it seem bizarre that drug companies are spending more money on convincing doctors of the benefits of prescription drugs rather than its consumers? In 2016, health care providers in the U.S. wrote more than 214 million prescriptions for opioid pain medication. It's alarming that every day, more than 1,000 people are treated in emergency departments for misusing prescription opioids. And of the roughly 214 million prescriptions, more than 40 percent of all US opioid overdose deaths in 2016 involved a prescription opioid.[7]

If such a large population of people is dying from drugs given to them by health care providers, the way our society uses drugs clearly needs serious revisions A drug is supposed to do more help than harm, not the other way around. However, shining some light on the toxicity associated with psychedelics, we come to an interesting conclusion. Deaths from psychedelics are so rare they aren't even visible when compared to deaths from tobacco and alcohol. Deaths from psychedelics account for roughly 0.000002 percent of a population in comparison to tobacco at 84.5 percent and alcohol at 15.5 percent.[8]

Take one of the more popular psychedelics, LSD, for example. "Physically, LSD is considered to be one of the least toxic drugs. Although lethal doses have been determined from experiments in several animal models, there has never been a recorded case of death exclusively attributed to LSD in humans".[9]

Drugs and our perception of what constitutes a tool have changed greatly in the last few decades.

Presented without their definitions, these terms seem completely unrelated, separated by societal unpopularity and misinterpreted through strict FDA regulations. Pre-adolescent degenerates consume illicit drugs, couch-locked individuals, banished from the polished order that defines our society. Why, then, are some of the most successful business entrepreneurs, CEOs, science innovators, and content creators consuming illicit chemicals daily? Specifically, why are they consuming some of the most controversial delicacies in all the world— LSD, MDMA, and psilocybin, to name a few? Notably, we see "technology stars, Steve Jobs and Bill Gates both famously experimenting with LSD" throughout their lives.[10]

Before Apple found its beginnings, Steve Jobs was a college dropout. He was not a motivational speaker, a sought-after CEO, or a publicly known big thinker. In his early twenties, the famous black turtleneck with a pair of loose blue jeans had yet to become trademarked. Instead, you would find twenty-some-year-old Jobs wearing a down jacket and walking around barefoot, only resorting to the bare minimum footwear, sandals, when it snowed. He lived in a "heatless garage apartment that he rented for $20 a month, returned soda bottles for spare change, and continued his treks to the free Sunday dinners at the Hare Krishna temple. When he needed money, he found work at the psychology department lab maintaining the electronic equipment that was used for animal behavior experiments."

So, how did a destitute Jobs, who abandoned his formal education in search of more interesting avenues, become one of the most well-known innovators and magnanimous entre-preneurs of the twenty-first century?

In an interview, Jobs states, ""I came of age at a magical time. Our consciousness was raised by Zen, and also by LSD'." Even later in life, he would credit psychedelic drugs for making him more enlightened. "'Taking LSD was a profound experience, one of the most important things in my life. LSD shows you that there's another side to the coin, and you can't remember it when it wears off, but you know it. It reinforced my sense of what was important—creating great things instead of making money, putting things back into the stream of history and of human consciousness as much as I could'".[11]

Perhaps it's time to remove the invisible walls that barricade our understanding of what drugs truly are, tools.

I say we forge a new concept that binds the definition of tools to drugs. And we need those tools to create the next great leap in human intelligence and capabilities.

SOFTWARE UPDATE, VERSION 2019

Mind Leap—a state of mind induced by a tool 'whose **particular function** is to **enhance physical or mental well-being.**

As we can see, with a bit of literary magic, we've produced something of interest. A **Mind Leap**. In computer science terms, this might be like updating the vintage Windows 1985 to a more modern, sleek, and refined Windows 10. If we think of the mind as a piece of computer software that mandates the functions of our body, we can begin to understand why all of this even matters and why some of the most successful people in the world are choosing to consume psychedelic substances.

In exploring how each of us can achieve a **Mind Leap** throughout this book, as a species, we can start to become more confident by understanding how much potential each of us has in achieving a desired role in society.

As humans, we have been fortunate enough to be passengers aboard this rocky spaceship we call Earth for over 2.6 million years, and humanity is now attempting to solve some of the largest problems in history.

Humanity has only occupied a small segment of time in the grand scheme of existence, so the question is, why now? Why did all these problems suddenly surface in the last few centuries?

This is where things get interesting. It's because we simply weren't aware that the problems existed. As humans, we excel at finding problems, and the more we evolve, the better this skill set becomes.

In the modern century, with the influx of exponential technologies, complex computer processing, and innovative data sensors, we have only further cultivated a society hyperaware of problems. And though we're aware that a problem exists, this doesn't mean we know how to solve it.

* * *

In the twenty-first century, we have seriously big ambitions.

If humanity wants to become an interplanetary species, solve climate change, refine our energy distribution systems, provide food and water for nearly eight billion humans, or adjust the various industries like education and the job market, we must be willing to change how we conceptualize problems. Especially as modern computing starts to work its way into the mind and hacks humans, those not constantly exploring new techniques to navigate through life will surely become mere cogs in the greater assembly of their social framework.

This book includes stories and insights to help us understand what is required to stay relevant and successful in our respective domains as we face ever-present threats by both technology and our environment.

- In Part I, Altered Minds, we explore why we should become more receptive to altered states of mind induced by psychedelics. This part loosely dives into the components of the mind and how it absorbs information from the world. Psychedelics are then introduced into the mix, revealing their potential to enhance and fortify human thought.

- After establishing a firm grounding for altered states, we then take a brief detour into humanity's relationship with psychedelics throughout the course of history in Part II, *Psychedelic Waves*. In Chapter 4, *Stoned Ape Hypothesis,* we will discuss specific stories about our ancestral past with psychedelics, and in Chapter 5, *Doors of Deception*, the rise of the counter-culture rebellion in the 1960s. These two eras mark the first two waves of the psychedelic revolution. Transitioning back into the present era, Chapter 6, *The Third Wave*, will then describe why we have now entered the third wave of the psychedelic revolution by shedding some light on its increasing popularity in the twenty-first century with a few relevant stories presented:

1. *Psychotherapists*
2. *High-performing Executives*
3. *Academics*

- Part III, *Mind Leap*, is then deliberated into three Chapters–each of which elucidates how to achieve an altered state of mind in alignment with the three categories above.

As of late, I have yet to see even one possible solution to charge toward our ambitions and save us from the grasps of exponential technologies' ability to hack us. If we want to solve any of these problems, we must be willing to undergo a Mind Leap, an internal software upgrade.

Now that you have the outline of the book, you may wonder how drugs can help us achieve a *Mind Leap.*

Or more elaborately, the *fundamental questions* this book attempts to answer are –

Can psychedelics collectively extend the cognitive space of humanity to enhance problem-solving capabilities and fortify mental resiliency?

More specifically, how can psychedelics be used to propel us into the next step of human evolution?

There's only one way to find out.

Let's redefine the way we think about drugs.

PART I

ALTERED MINDS

CHAPTER 1

CULTURAL POISONS

———

"They've identified these receptors in the brain that activate specific circuits. And you know how they say that we can only access 20 percent of our brain? Well, what this does... it lets you access all of it.

Vern, look at me. Do I look good to you? I'm broke and I'm depressed off my ass. I don't think that my life's gonna take some sudden upswing into fame and fortune by taking some shiny, brand-new designer drug."

—LIMITLESS[12]

Taking drugs to enhance how you navigate through life is nothing new. In Hollywood's best-seller, *Limitless*, we've seen this perspective before, which proposed the ultimate chemical recipe to enhance both your cognitive and social abilities. With just one pill a day, climbing to the top of humanity's social hierarchy becomes all too easy.

Now, I'm not one to believe in mythical fantasies.

Anyone who tells you there's *one chemical to rule them all* is completely delusional. No one-time, cure-all, magic drug can solve all the world's problems. But time and time again, this idea starts to boil up within our social atmosphere, especially when it comes to psychedelics or, in the case of *Limitless*, NZT.

In *Limitless*, the movie's protagonist finds himself in one of the most precarious positions of his life. He's broke and jobless, the love of his life just dumped him, and he can't even muster up the focus to write a single word for his *"sci-fi novel, a personal manifesto about the plight of the individual"."* Disheveled and wreaking of alcohol and cigarettes, a depressed Eddie then reaches his lowest low. However, just as he's about to tip over the edge into homelessness, something happens. He bumps into his ex-girlfriend's brother, who apparently found the quick fix Eddie needs to turn his life around. Waving a small bag with a tiny cylindrical pill inside, he then offers Eddie a brand-new research chemical known as NZT.

NZT offers its users a way out of their complacency, their every-day powerlessness to achieve their most compelling dreams. Hesitantly, Eddie accepts his offer and takes the drug. A few moments after it's consumed, Eddie is then propelled into an *altered state of mind*, unlike anything he has ever experienced. Popping one pill a day, he finishes his sci-fi novel in just four days, lands one of the most valuable stock-broker positions on Wall Street, and builds a portfolio of stocks worth millions. And, for the cherry on top, he gets the love of his life back in his arms.

But, if there were no downsides to the chemical, it wouldn't make for much a movie. Eddie finds out after taking NZT for months that, with all the amazing benefits it offers, without it, the body suffers from severe withdraws, leading many of its users to their deaths. To avoid spoiling the movie, I'll stop right there.

Transitioning back into reality, clearly, there is no chemical quite like NZT. But the movie communicates rather that while drugs have the potential to leap us into more effective states of mind, we should still be hyper-conscientious of their dangers. At the end of the day, drugs are toxins. They are foreign substances that can negatively impact the building blocks of our biology. Innately, however, the human-animal is still drawn to **mind-altering** chemicals regardless of their fundamental downsides or probable neurotoxicity.

If some entity can be used to amplify how someone feels or how they communicate, chances are, they will gravitate toward it. Stemming from its tremendous sense of pride among other selective pressures in the environment, the human-animal is a highly competitive creature. And after Charles Darwin's work was published in the late nineteenth century, this idea has only been further embraced. We now refer to our continual attempts to feel or think *better (among many other components)* as a product of *natural selection.*

Our innate attraction to toxins is just another avenue we can use to hone our competitive edge. For example, when we think of vaccines, we usually think of them as being **medicinal substances** for preventing future disease. More broadly, another interpretation of a vaccine might be to view it as a solution of toxins, customized and **attenuated*** to fulfill a specific purpose within the **human** body. This is the fundamental insight that sparked the creation of vaccines. When Edward Jenner developed the first successful vaccine in 1796, he discovered that *a toxin is not inherently poisonous, but rather dependent on the host that consumes it.*

He observed that dairymaids who caught a virus in the same family of smallpox from cows, known as cowpox, developed an immunity to smallpox. While cows that caught cowpox generally had a low rate of survivability, a human infected by cowpox had a high rate. This is because the cowpox virus has evolved based on a cow's immune system, not a human. For this reason, unlike smallpox, the cowpox virus became an opponent our immune system could takedown–in which it could then create the necessary antibodies not only for cowpox but also similar viruses like smallpox.[13]

Nowadays, getting vaccines has become a cultural norm in America. Among many types of vaccines given, roughly 85 percent of the American population receives them.[14] And it's no wonder why. Two doses of the chickenpox vaccine are 90 percent effective at preventing chickenpox, two doses of the measles vaccine – 97 percent, HPV vaccine – almost one hundred percent, and the list goes on and on. Not getting a vaccine is not only risky but also irresponsible, as it increases the chances for a virus to spread.[1]

But even though we're aware of their benefits, we must not forget that a vaccine, just like psychedelics, is a toxin. Of course, they have wildly different effects, with vaccines geared toward altering the body and psychedelics—altering the mind, nonetheless, both are foreign entities that play significant roles within the confines of human biology.

Keep in mind, this does not mean that what vaccines are for the body, psychedelics are for the mind. Partly because psychedelic research is still heavily restricted, no preliminary evidence eludes to this idea. Regardless, we **should** be willing to recognize that psychedelics introduces a state of mind that can be extremely effective in *enhancing* and *fortifying* our waking state of mind.

OCEAN MOOD

Interestingly, it's highly controversial to make a claim like this in America. After all, psychedelics are illegal. But when we look at modern medicine, it's even more fascinating when we hone our attention to the current medicines widely prescribed to strengthen the mind.

For example, one of the most commonly used anti-depressant medications are called SSRIs (Selective Serotonin Reuptake Inhibitor). The general thinking behind SSRI treatment is that depressed individuals have decreased levels of a chemical messenger called serotonin in the brain (or more commonly known as *the happiness molecule*). When a patient begins consuming SSRIs, they "are thought to work by increasing levels of serotonin in the brain, but nobody knows for certain." (Note: Any time a substance targets a nerve ending that releases chemical messengers, such as serotonin, we add the root word, -ergic, meaning 'sensitive to'. In this case, SSRIs would be known as **serotonergic** substances).

However, of the nearly 30 million people currently taking anti-depressant medications in the U.S., only 20 percent of them will show *improved* symptoms.[16] And if these people are using the most common anti-depressants, on average, they will spend nearly $200 for a full cycle of treatment. Or another way to frame it—roughly **$4 billion** is wasted each year on anti-depressant medication in America.[17] It's not a stunning conclusion either. Many psychiatrists are aware of the infectivity of mood-disorder therapies.

As John Geddes, a professor of psychiatry at Oxford University, says, "*We don't have any very precise treatments for depression at this point in time.*" In other words, SSRIs, among many other anti-depressants, are still the most viable option for treating mood disorders. It's no wonder that many experts say, "New treatments are badly needed".[18] Although we can point fingers at modern medicine's shortcomings, it doesn't help alleviate our situation, especially if our claims lack an alternative. However, psychedelics may have the potential to remedy this problem – just not in the traditional way one might think.

For instance, psychedelics, just like most modern anti-depressant medications, are primarily serotonergic, but the claim to replace anti-depressants with psychedelics is not because of this. Modern neuroscience research is still in the **black-box phase**, in which many mechanisms of psychoactive substances remain unknown. Even though thousands of neuroscience papers are published each year, no piece of science literature has explained the exact correlation between serotonin and mood-disorders.

Simply put, neuroscience is in the Dark Age when it comes to elucidating the functions of the brain. With the knowledge available, it's impossible to make a definitive statement like those that claim treating mood-disorders is simply a matter of manipulating serotonin levels.

To further this idea, peering into the work produced by David Nichols, a professor at Purdue University, might help us adjust our perceptions about the current state of modern neuroscience.

Attempting to transition neuroscience from the dark age to the renaissance, in 1993, Dr. Nichols founded *The Heffter Research Institute (HRI),* one of the only large-scale facilities researching classic psychedelic compounds. According to his predictions, we are still thirty to forty years away from designing drugs with a specific function in mind. In other words, drug discovery is still in its infant stages.

Whether it be an anti-depressant or a *smart drug,* the route to synthesize non-toxic chemicals is a lot like finding a needle in the haystack. It takes years of work to find one shiny, new chemical that may have a beneficial impact on the human psyche. We will revisit this idea in later Chapters, but the key thing to keep in mind is that psychedelics serotonergic behavior has not necessarily caused this class of substances to become the subject of much debate in society.

These chemicals may be wildly beneficial for our species not because of their ability to treat a *specific* mood-disorder but, rather, their ability to put us into an altered state of consciousness **entirely foreign** from our normal waking state. In turn, just after one experience with a dose high enough to trigger a *psychedelic experience*, the human psyche is dramatically influenced.

To understand the magnitude of this influence, researchers at the Imperial College of London measured twenty patients' personalities before and after they received the drug psilocybin, which is the active psychoactive compound inside many types of fungi now called *magic mushrooms*. After receiving a dose of 10 milligrams (mg) and 25mg, one week apart, they observed something incredibly fascinating when their patients returned three months later.

The *'Big Five'* Personality Traits (*OCEAN*)[19] are composed of:

- *Openness (O)* – indicates how open-minded and authority challenging a person is.
- *Conscientiousness (C)* – indicates how self-disciplined and organized a person is.
- *Extraversion (E)* – indicates how outgoing and social a person is.
- *Agreeableness (A)* – indicates how warm, friendly, and tactful a person is.
- *Neuroticism (N)* – indicates a person's ability to remain stable and balanced.

The researchers found that *Neuroticism* decreased; Extraversion, *Conscientiousness,* and *Openness* all increased; and *Agreeableness* remained unchanged.[20] (O⁺, C⁺, E⁺, A°, N*)

In other words, we see that psilocybin has the power to increase our mind's ability to embrace intellectual curiosity (O⁺), socialize with others (E⁺), and maintain mental fortitude (C⁺) while also decreasing the volatility of moods and our tendency to get stuck in negative ones (N*).

These results are intriguing because after reaching age 21, throughout the normal maturation of the human-animal, we find that in:

- Males—C and E increase while O and A decrease (O**, C⁺⁺, E⁺, A**, N°).

- Females—C increases while A decreases (O°, C⁺⁺, E°, A**, N°). [21]

Now that we have a bit of information about what psychedelics does to our personality, and how our personality changes over time, I want to challenge you to think for a moment.

**NOTE:

(+) (+ +) –denotes increasingly positive change.

(*) (**) – denotes increasingly negative change.

(o) – denotes little or no change.

If everyone added one of these psychedelic experiences to their repertoire, what impacts could this have on:

1. *The Individual*
2. *Your Immediate Community*
3. *Your Extended Community (**Society**)*

- Don't be afraid to write it down, both good and bad *short-term* and *long-term* effects. It might be helpful to sketch out each of these categories by using the following graph. Here's an example for the individual:

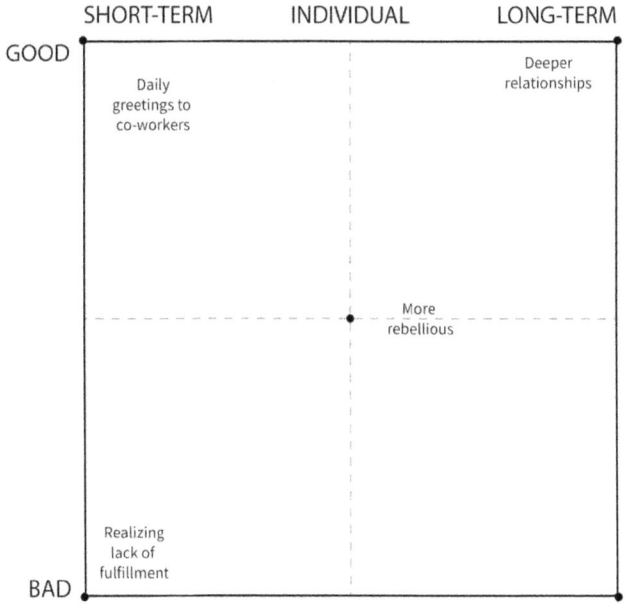

* * *

Now, when we consider once more why psychedelics may be an effective way to treat mood disorders, it's less about psychedelics being the direct solution and more that it provides the means to make micro-adjustments within our lives. By slightly changing who we are at our core and with a bit of responsibility, psychedelics can become tools to propagate thoughtful waves of change. 'An old Chinese proverb outlines this idea better:

For want of a nail, the shoe was lost
For want of a shoe, the horse was lost
For want of a horse, the rider was lost
For want of a rider, the battle was lost
For want of a battle, the kingdom was lost!

In western culture, this idea is known as the *Butterfly Effect*, in which the smallest changes make the biggest impacts on the world. Psychedelics are very similar in this nature, and as we will find out, when we change our sense of self at a fundamental level, it gives us the opportunity to upgrade the mind, or in the case of mood disorders, regain its control.

If we conceptualize life for a moment as this sort of infinite body of water and the human body as the ship that allows us passage through it, personality and its resulting mind is nothing more than a loose guide to steer the rudder. As the waves of reality smash into the ship, without the proper motivation or purpose, the rudder becomes frail and manip-ulatable. And as supplies dwindle when lost in life's currents, a sense of direction escapes, and the ship starts to break down. And very quickly, we start to notice how easily mood disorders can develop.

However, we often forget that the strength and tensile of the ship, the supplies that provide support on the journey, and the knowledge gained about steering the rudder came from somewhere. In other words, we must add another element to the mix, the most important one of them all that drastically effects where each journey leads and how well-equipped one is when life throws bigger waves. While each journey may be dynamic in nature, it seems that many of us have lost sight of where we've come from and the impact it's played in determining where we're going. The ship and the ability to steer the rudder are the products of a much greater entity. Mood disorders are no different.

SOCIAL POISONS

Generally, when mood disorders are brought up in con-versation, we tend to focus on the common ones like *depression, anxiety, and PTSD,* among a few others. They are the tileable suburbs, the overwatered lawns, and the hybrid cars that fill up society. They are symptoms of a much deeper social phenomenon called **culture**. And without deliberate introspection, it's easy to fall victim to the flow of culture and become attached to its ideas and its resulting mindsets.

As we consider how culture plays a role in determining how an individual operates, we may come to realize that culture is another form of A.I., molded by a collection of minds and unconsciously shaping the minds of those under its spell. Because of its complexity, culture is very difficult to explain. 'It must be experienced and becomes hardwired in the mind after living in a place for an extended period. It's the same idea when it comes to mood disorders or any altered state of mind like those mentioned previously.

We can describe the general components that make a culture what it is, or how being depressed or anxious feels, but still, we hit a dead-end when it comes to recreating the exact scenario that led to the evolution of a culture and the subsequent mind states within it.

For example, nearly 5,000 years ago in ancient Egyptian culture, humanity saw the birth of one of the most astonishing technologies, The Egyptian Pyramids. For nearly one hundred years, Egyptians employed thousands of workers and hauled millions of tons of raw material to create these brilliant structures. It's bizarre, however, that after years of work building a pyramid, and surely countless lives lost, they would cease progression and move their entire operation to a new location to build their next great landmark.

There have been countless discussions about why numerous pyramids were built, instead of just one, and why each of Giza's pyramids are oriented to face the four cardinal directions: true north, south, east, and west. Some theorize that pyramids may have been used to generate energy from nearby water sources, some say it was due to spiritual reasons, and others, like archeologist Marian Cook, say that "the evolution of all the pyramids was the result of these practical *what-if* experiments. The ancient Egyptians became increasingly ambitious, testing the limits of their skills and their raw materials".[22]

With new theories being conjured each year, it's quite clear that the mysteries of the Egyptian pyramids remain. Regardless of the true reason for building these pyramids, much of the underlying evolutionary mechanics behind a culture's decisions are opaque to those outside of it. The same holds true when we try to elucidate the evolutionary framework of mood disorders. They have deep roots well nested below the surface of what's communicable to outsiders, but it doesn't have to be that way. Cultural communication is the key here, because without communicating with ourselves, how in the world do we expect to communicate as a collective?

Are we to fall into the same trap as our Egyptian ancestors, only to build some magnificent-grand-standing structure or society in the world, filled with our deepest insights, and then watch as later humans stumble around in our ruins asking themselves the same questions we ask about the Egyptian Pyramids?

DIGITAL MASKS

Nowadays, it's quite clear that with the rise of the digital revolution, connective technologies like social media and the internet have only catalyzed our insufficient ability to truly look inward—to take time for deep introspective work and upgrade the conversational dialogue within our own minds. With the bombardment of "breaking news" and the influx of advertisements, our culture's attention span has diminished in the last few decades. Also, it is well known that a dangerous correlation exists between social media and mental health.

"For example, individuals who *spend more time on social media and less time with others face-to-face* report *lower well-being* and are *more likely to be depressed*".[23]

And it's not just an individual effort. Those in control of social platforms are just as responsible as those who choose to use them. As Cal Newport writes in his book, *Digital*

Minimalism, "The tycoons of social media have to stop pretending that *they're friendly nerd gods building a better world* and *admit they're just tobacco farmers in T-shirts selling an addictive product to children.* Because, let's face it, checking your 'likes' is the new smoking."[24]

Every day, I find myself constantly unsubscribing from some email chain or job marketing scandal only to wonder how many others are also waking up each day to find their 'emails littered with the same scraps of information?

While online, it's easy to get caught in the monotonous black and whites of the internet, constantly hearing people brag about their decorated wall of achievements or complaining about so-and-so politician, scrolling through Instagram or Facebook feeds only to see how much time and effort people take to make an artificial version of themselves. For the most part, the online world has stimulated the creation of an entirely false version of the self. Culturally defined by the number of 'likes' or 'shares' they receive, people have started to align themselves not with their own interpretation of who they are but by the digital masks drafted by others.

In 2019, it is projected that people will spend almost seven years on social media in their lifetime. In addition, people will spend triple the amount of time "connecting" on social media as they do face-to-face. After all, the "me" online is much easier to hide behind. The internet is a way of pulling a curtain over people's eyes, to block our own deepest insecurities and vulnerabilities from seeing the light of day.

However, revealing vulnerabilities is one of the most essential components of communicating. When we restrict our abilities to do so, we lose that crucial component of authenticity that allows us to excel in the world. In an interview with Gay Gaddis, the owner and founder of T3 (The Think Tank) in Austin, TX, she realized on her twenty-three-year-long pursuit to become what is now the largest advertising agency wholly owned by a woman that, "When you shut down vulnerability, you shut down opportunity–Entrepreneurship is all about vulnerability".[25]

The problem with social media is that, if abused, it becomes challenging to embrace this idea. With little restrictions on social media, we are seeing its toll on mental health.

After conducting a nationwide survey of more than 600,000 U.S. kids between the ages of twelve and seventeen, researchers at Columbia University found that rates of depression have risen from 8.7 percent in 2005 to 12.7 percent in 2015.[26] And when we look at stress or anxiety levels of individuals in this age group, another study found that the number of Facebook friends directly correlates to an increase in daily cortisol levels, the stress hormone.[27] At a time most crucial for the development of their communication abilities, children have been lured into the cultural trap of social media. Probably stemming from constant social media use, among other factors, human loneliness is also on the rise.

A 2017 report by the HRSA declares the emergence of a loneliness epidemic finding that "two in five Americans report that they sometimes or always feel their social relationships are not meaningful, and one in five say they feel lonely or socially isolated".[28]

To avoid being called a soundbite journalist, I won't just outline the negatives. Social Media is not purely a maniacal, demonic entity that feeds on negative emotions. By rethinking how to use it, we must realize that it can increase our ability to communicate.

"For instance, a study of 1,839 college students by Reynol Junco at Lock Haven University in the US found that using Facebook for collecting and sharing information was positively predictive of GPA – suggesting that, like most technologies, Facebook use can have some good as well as negative impacts".[29]

In using it as a supplementary medium to communicate, not a primary one, social media platforms can be used effectively. However, after becoming dependent on these platforms, making this shift is much easier said than done. Left to its own devices and comforted by social media's accessibility, the human mind becomes resistance to changing its course. However, with a slight adjustment to the mind, perhaps we can alleviate its stubbornness. Reading a few articles or books on how to get in the *right mindset* is not what we need. The problem does not come from a lack of information from the outside but rather a lack of information about the inside of our minds and the self-discipline to explore its depths.

Absorbing information is only as effective as the mind that allows it to do so. Tapping into altered states of consciousness is necessary because, clearly, an intense **communication deficit** is transpiring within many modern minds, one that may be fixable with a slight priority adjustment.

And we see it not only restricting our social abilities but also our problem-solving capabilities.

CHAPTER 2

EXPONENTIAL MINDS

———

Whether we like to admit it or not, by nature, we are an incredibly gifted species at solving problems. We've been able to dig miles under the ground to find a wealth of energy sources that we can distribute to entire societies, excelling growth and drastically increasing physiological comfort with indoor climate control and efficient transportation. We've flown miles above the ground to launch spaceship satellites that monitor large-scale terrestrial problems and help us navigate whenever we get lost with modern GPS technologies.

As we transitioned into the era of digitalization and complex computer processing, we've even created entire arsenals of online learning and connective technologies. Effectively, we have built the largest framework of human minds, the likes of which human history has never seen before. And from a neurological perspective, there's one major theory of why the human-animal is so good at solving problems and why it is the dominant species on Earth. The human brain has a reward system unlike any other species.

THE ORIGINS OF MOTIVATION

Neurologically, we have been hardwired to crave that ubiquitous "**ah-ha**" moment—that feeling when we can finally shout "**Eureka!**" That excitement we feel every time we collect a new insight or find an alternative way to solve a problem truly sets us apart from other species. The great divide between humans and apes millions of years ago may have been caused by a chemical called *dopamine*, the chemical messenger that plays a key role in the human brain's reward system.[30]

To test this theory, researchers in Austria conducted a study in which thirty participants were asked to solve a collection of word puzzles. They were shown three words and were required to come up with one new word associated with all three.

For example, they were given the words, "house", "bark", and "apple".

Think for a minute—what word would you choose?

If you thought "tree", Congratulations!

If you successfully solved this word puzzle, you probably noticed a short moment of pleasure. That's because a small amount of dopamine was just released in your brain, according to the results of the study. In other words, we must thank *dopamine* for our continual desire to solve problems and achieve more. People who say they're extremely "self-motivated" may just be those who've learned how to *hack* the concentration of dopamine inside their brains. They won't tell you they're also consuming copious amounts of cocaine, Adderall, and coffee, psychoactive stimulants that enhance dopamine signaling in the brain.[31]

There's a reason *hyper-productive* investment bankers and stockbrokers have notorious ties to cocaine. "Cocaine and investment banking have been best friends since the 1980s when Wall Street's rise in popular culture and London's Big Bang created wealth and the envy of having/not having wealth." Wanting to achieve more, make more, and rise to the top, cocaine use became an activity to stimulate and reinforce greed with pleasure.

Brought on by their substance abuse, the internal mechanism that drives motivation became obsolete and reliant on external sources to do the same trick. Guided by "the stress of their work and uncertain futures," investment banking became a job for "the educated white boy to [sling] crack rock".[32]

However, even though cocaine has a bad *rep*, we must keep in mind that, like any drug, it is still a tool—a wildly addictive one—but a tool, nonetheless. We briefly alluded to the idea that humans are innately attracted to drugs in Chapter 1, but we can really explore this idea at greater lengths now that we have two neurotransmitters to play with, *dopamine* and *serotonin*. We may find more to the story when we try to explain our relationship to these toxins and why we continue to consume them.

DRUG PARADOX THEORY

When we think of a drug like SSRIs, mentioned in Chapter 1, or cocaine, we consider these chemicals toxins or poisons not just because they're foreign entities. To say that a drug like SSRI works by increasing serotonin levels in the brain is only partially true.

In theory, SSRI-type drugs work by *inhibiting* the *re-uptake* of serotonin from the outside of a cell, *extracellular*, to the inside of a cell, *intracellular*. They do this by *selecting* a specific type of protein on the cell's surface known as a receptor, essentially a chemical floodgate, and binding to it – hence *selective serotonin re-uptake inhibitor*.

We think of these chemicals as toxins because they're blocking specific pathways chemicals can take in our brain. Intuitively, it might seem that closing the dam, the receptor, would only harm an individual because the brain can't perform its normal functions. But it's not as if the brain just suddenly shuts down (*not in the case of inhibiting one site at least*). Millions of pathways inside the brain will still perform normal activities. However, once the serotonin receptor is blocked, suddenly, serotonin is trapped intracellularly, effectively changing our neurochemistry for a short period.

Dr. Hagen and Dr. Sullivan produced an interesting theory in 2002, formally known as the *Drug Paradox,* about 'humans' relationship to drugs and their unique neurobiology. In other words, there must be some reason we use these substances because we didn't evolve to poison ourselves.

These poisons do change our neurochemistry, and that's precisely the point.

Just drink a cup of coffee, and you'll see what I mean – This toxin is consumed daily, and yet millions of humans drink it because they like how it **communicates** with their body and its subsequent effects on their performance.

In other words, we consume drugs because they change how we **communicate** both **internally** and **externally.**

When we revisit cocaine, it's quite clear that the way we communicate becomes drastically different. We become energized, motivated, and sometimes rather aggressive. However, when viewing these chemicals from a plant's perspective (*in the case of cocaine, the coca plant*), these chemicals were not specifically designed to alter human behavior in this way. Many animals die when they consume coca leaves. Dr. Hagen and Dr. Sullivan's describe this phenomenon as merely a *coincidence*.

They point out that, "From the perspective of evolutionary ecology, plants **should not have evolved defensive chemicals** that **easily trigger reward in consumers**, and consumers **should not have evolved neural circuitry** that **readily but inadvertently rewards** or **reinforces consumption** of numerous neurotoxins."

After studying various chemicals like nicotine (tobacco), cocaine (coca), and caffeine (coffee), among many others, they discovered a *"long-term evolutionary relationship between psychotropics and humans"*.[33]

Even more so, they realized humans had evolved a unique set of neurotransmitters designed from the selective pressures of plant toxins. In other words, the evolution of the human-animal intersects with drug consumption, and the brain started to adapt and **use plants as a source of neurotransmitters**. By creating chemicals like dopamine and serotonin, which are highly reactive to many substances in our environment, the

human-animal could then become more adaptable because it could use plants as a source of dopamine and serotonin, among many other neurotransmitters, to maintain its competitive advantage over other species.

Evolutionarily, this makes a lot of sense. If we ask why an organism would want to consume drugs whenever they face problems, we can figure this out by briefly detouring into the hunter-gatherer era of our species.

In this era, the human-animal thrived because that same feeling we get when we solve a word problem also occurs when we hunt down an animal. In turn, this would then motivate primitive communities to volunteer to go hunting. And just like that–dopamine provides us with a pleasurable reward so that the pain and exhaustion usually associated with gathering food now becomes a desirable activity.

For this reason, dopamine is a very powerful chemical because it (*primarily*) serves two purposes. First, it motivates us to solve a problem (*collecting food*) and, second, solving a problem usually supported the survival of our species (*providing food*).

However, as we've evolved, so, too, has the very nature of our problems. This is where the *Drug Paradox Theory* comes into play. To get to where we are today, early Homo sapiens had to figure out how to solve harder and harder problems—like how to track down *smarter* animals or defend against *stronger* ones to get their daily dose of dopamine.

For example, around 9000 B.C., before the formation of the first civilizations, we see strong historical evidence of psilocybin, *magic mushrooms*, being used by cultures when we view vivid cave paintings glorifying them.

And this is just the first documented appearance of psychedelic usage. Perhaps a much lesser-known use of psychedelics might have been their application while hunting.[34]

Physiologically, the human body becomes more receptive to the environment a couple of hours after consuming magic mushrooms. Along with an increase in heart rate and mental energy, colors begin to become more vibrant, sounds become sharper, and the perception of time begins to slow down.[35]

As a hunter, being able to distinguish and lock onto animals well-camouflaged in their natural environment is a highly valuable trait. In addition, depending on the size and speed of the prey in sight, mental exhaustion might rapidly poison the human's desire to pursue the prey further as high-focus situations require meditative concentration to keep still and not make a sound.

Inserting psilocybin into this situation, perhaps a mediocre hunter can then accomplish his task. By recognizing patterns with a much higher level of competency and cadence and increasing his endurance, the hunter can then capture or kill the animal target and receive the desired bump of dopamine.

By changing the hunter's perceptions, harder problems and tasks became easier. And as time went on, the better the hunter, the more likely he would reproduce. In other words, perhaps the hunters who consumed these types of drugs were the ones from which modern humans draw their genetics. When it comes to psilocybin, however, this idea still lacks significant scientific evidence.

However, an article published in 2008 by a team of researchers at Hertfordshire Partnership University claims that "one could think that ancestors who tolerated and benefited from moderate/limited drug use may have had other selective advantages such as pain relief obtained with opiates, or increased energy with stimulants. This could have been useful during hunt, foraging or situations requiring physical endurance or privation".[36]

So, when it comes to solving problems, humans use of drugs both ancestrally and presently is well-known. But the problems of the modern era are much more complex than the problems our ancestors faced.

Hunting animals is a rather useless activity these days because most of the livestock we use for food are now domesticated and surrounded by barbed wire fences. Even more so, the modernization of hunting tools, transforming bows into rifles, has removed much of the challenges associated with hunting.

Wired by our innate tendencies to receive bursts of dopamine, many humans no longer seek hunting as a rewarding activity for these reasons. Instead of animals, we now can track globalized problems like climate change, economic regression, and mental aptitude. In these domains, plenty of problems remain, and when we do solve them, we can get that subsequent pleasurable sensation our ancestors felt after a successful day of hunting.

However, before you gear up and go out to solve these problems to get your daily fix of dopamine, remember that no one has solved the many remaining problems within these fields.

It's not necessarily that we don't have enough data either. With the advance of technology and computational sciences fields, we have more data than we know what to do with! More information about the world we live in doesn't necessarily facilitate a better understanding of it or tell us how to solve the problems within it. What we lack is not cognitive power, but cognitive originality.

"We cannot solve our problems with the same level of think-
ing that created them".

—ALBERT EINSTEIN

In other words, when humans become aware of a problem
or realize that a problem has developed, we can't solve it just
by collecting more and more data; we also need to apply a
level of thinking that goes beyond our current capabilities.

For example, in Matt Mcarthy's book, *Superbugs*, he
details one of the up and coming *exponential* problems
of the twenty-first century—globalized outbreaks of infec-
tious diseases. The general idea is that we aren't the only
ones evolving. While hospitals supplemented our immune
system with antibiotic drugs like penicillin, effectively
protecting a large majority of people from airborne bacteria (*microbes*), Mcarthy proposes that this may not be
the case in the modern era.

He states, "To understand how this is possible, we might
invoke the infinite monkey theorem, which argues that a
monkey hitting keys at random on a computer keyboard for
an infinite amount of time will eventually produce coherent
text, including the complete works of William Shakespeare.
By way of comparison, microbes are constantly mutating,
hitting the proverbial keys in novel combinations, and those

sequences produce enzymes and pumps that can deflect or destroy any antibiotic."

In other words, from the many subsequent generations of failed mutant microbes, there may arise a victor powerful enough to become one of the world's biggest problems–a superbug. This idea has bounced around different disciplines, and then in 1995, "the era of genomic medicine had finally arrived," or so they thought.

A group of forty scientists, led by Craig Venter, could now sequence the entire genome of species of bacterium (known as *Haemophilus Influenzae)*, and so you might leap to the same conclusions that they did. More information about a species genome, essentially a vast ocean of data, would help serve "as a template *to develop all sorts of drugs that had once been unimaginable.*" But they made one major miscalculation. Although Venter's team sequenced a bacteria's genome, they were unable to solve the superbug problem.

Over six years, almost half a million compounds were screened with this template in mind. However, Mcarthy continues, "The program proved to be a massive failure. Using Venter's genetic information to screen for antibiotics had been a big waste of time and prompted a radical shift in corporate strategy. The debacle set drug discovery back a generation, if not more, and the field still hasn't recovered." [37]

Now, I'm not saying this information was worthless—rather, information can become extremely valuable, but first humans must interpret it. For example, there's a well-known reason why humans and non-human primates are extremely sensitive to snakes and can detect them with a high level of aptitude. Early hominids were a timid and fragile bunch, unable to compete in strength against carnivorous "big" cats and other prehistoric animal giants; our species found their place among the trees.

And we weren't the only ones in the trees.

Slithering among the branches, snakes became one of our primary foes.

But it's not snakes who rule the world these days.

While we're unaware of the exact route that led us to be able to detect snakes and their unique camouflage signatures, we know that according to the *Snake Detection Theory*, humans evolved an acute visual system specifically designed to "*recognize snakes under less discernible visual conditions*" "more accurately than non-threatening animals (*e.g., birds, cats or fish*)" as pointed out by Nobuyuki Kawai at Nagoya University.

In other words, at some point, humans could turn a snake's **visual information** (*color* patterns) into **visual knowledge** ("that's a snake!"). By adding this snake detection component to the human visual system, they could then react *quickly*, before they met their demise with potential *slithering encounters*.

Even more so, as snake camouflage evolved and subsequently, by allocating some of the human brain's resources to this specific organism, deciphering snakes was no longer a problem. This is why people in the modern era intuitively detect snakes better than any other animal. It's hardwired in the human brain![38]

Long story short, we built a dynamic interpretation system (one that changed with snakes), so we could ensure the survival of our species.

The opposite is true when we look at heaps of genetic data. We've been unable to decipher the dynamic nature of **genetic information** (*gene* patterns). In turn, transforming this information into **genetic knowledge** ("Let's use antibiotic A instead of B!") is extremely challenging because we have not evolved to **consciously** interpret bacterium quickly. Instead, our immune system does it for us **unconsciously**, which enables quick interpretation for the individual, while sacrificing quick distribution for the collective.

So, when we attempt to communicate these massive sets of information through conscious mediums like writing and speaking, which inherently take time to formulate and distribute, the initial state of information bears little similarity with its present state. By the time we sequence genetic information, it's already outdated and the bacterium has evolved! For the same reason we don't look at cavemen to draw specific conclusions about modern Homo sapiens, we shouldn't use genetic information to draw specific conclusions about how to make novel antibiotics (so long as our present communication medium remains unchanged).

In other words, information has a half-life. In order to crack the genetic code, we need an adaptive interpretation system, not a stagnant one.

After all, genetics, let alone computer processing of genetics, is an extremely new field and, at least in viewing Venter's work, we have not built this dynamic interpretation system...**yet**.

When it comes to pattern recognition, we clearly won't be able to recognize patterns quickly enough unless we literally change how our neurochemistry communicates information. While we can perhaps use computers for this function, the problem is that we are still the ones programming them. We can make computer software that learns based on present information, but without understanding how bacterium mutates, we may find that many of the up and coming *machine-learning algorithms (A.I.)* are worthless unless they know *how* to learn—not *what* to learn.

When we analyze data, it's the same idea. Therefore, analyzing *what* information means is only valuable when we also analyze *how* that information changes. As we target larger and larger data pools, as in the case of genetics, the scope of data approaches exponential change. In other words, to solve these problems, we need to unlock the mind's ability to start thinking *exponentially.*

EXPONENTIAL THINKING

Revisiting the *Snake Detection Theory*, we may find that a different balance of neurotransmitters was needed—perhaps, one influenced by the *"higher-level cognitive, perceptual, and affective effects of serotonergic hallucinogens"*.[39]

When I told you that psychedelics are primarily serotonergic, I wasn't being entirely truthful. Serotonergic hallucinogens are also glutamatergic (stimulating glutamate). Interestingly much of the human visual system is mandated by two specific neurotransmitters, GABA and *Glutamate*. *"By altering the concentrations of the two neurotransmitters, the brain is able to process visual stimuli from the eyes"*.[40] In other words, psychedelic's glutamatergic nature may be one of the primary reasons for the *visual* effects associated with psychedelics.

So, if we teleported back in time, we might find humans who can detect snake camouflage and those who can't might have a clear differentiation in how these two neurotransmitters operate.

But the curious question is, did our ability to evolve a visual system that could detect snakes arise from our use of psychedelics?

While the answer to this question is still unknown, if we apply this idea to modern-day problem solving, it's easy to see how this could be beneficial. By upgrading the conceptual abilities through which we create our interpretations about the world, the difficulty of problems we set out to achieve starts to decrease.

However, this is still just a hypothesis. But when we start thinking of psychedelics in this way, we realize exponential thinking is not outside our reach but just a neurochemical manipulation away. However, there's one more component to worry about when it comes to tackling big problems. The external world is not the only one changing exponentially, so is the human species.

CHAPTER 3

THOUGHTWARE

———

Personality and *Culture*

Information and *Knowledge*

The *Mind* and *Neurochemistry*

We've brought up many ideas in the last few Chapters, like—

- How *personality* and *culture* are really two sides of the same coin in Chapter 1.

- How *information* and *knowledge* are essential components for solving problems in Chapter 2.

- How the state of the *mind* reacts when we change our *neurochemistry,* as we saw in both Chapters.

The primary goal of this Chapter is to reveal how all these topics are interwoven into the mental fabric of our minds. We will now build a basic conceptual framework to help us understand the primary value of altered states of consciousness induced by psychedelics. With these topics serving as building blocks, we will glue them together, effectively constructing one way to view the mind—a type of software known as *Thoughtware.*

By understanding the doors of perception embedded inside this *Thoughtware,* our abilities to undergo a *Mind Leap* will start to become more apparent.

GENERATIONAL SOFTWARE

Synthetic evolution, brought on by the development of technology, is growing much faster and more complex every day. In comparison to our own organic evolution, we might find that if we continue down the path toward mental stagnancy, technology will continue to consume our minds and change how we think and how society operates. Or as Harari mentioned previously, humans are increasingly becoming *hackable* animals.

In Chapter 1, we saw how the rise of the technology from the digital revolution is hacking many individual's communication abilities. In Chapter 2, we saw how our deficiencies in solving big problems arise from our inability to synthesize information and create *adaptive* knowledge with the influx of large sets of data like genetic information.

When we frame it like this, it might be easier to draw a correlation. How we communicate socially directly impacts how we communicate in our work lives. If we want to regain control of our lives and solve harder and harder problems, we must realize how imperative it is to change how we communicate as a species and with the world we inhabit.

The human mind is one of the most complex pieces of software we've ever encountered, and yet we neglect how powerful it can become when we change our diets, get some exercise, or—sorry, America—take drugs. If we want to solve the world's most challenging problems, we must be willing to change how this internal software interprets information and generates knowledge.

We are already seeing the next generations of human *Thoughtware* taking downward turns into social isolation and mood degradation. This version of the human-animal's *generational software* is more commonly referred to as **Millennials (1977-1994)** or **Gen-Z (1995-2012)**, individuals who have grown up with overarching influences of technologies in the digital revolution.

From the time they've entered the known, the information and technologies present in the environment have made incomparable impacts (*relative to other generations*) on how they feel, where they want to work, and what problems they want to solve. It's only becoming more clear as books about social media abuse (like *The Coddling of the American Mind* by Jonathon Haidt and Greg Lukianoff or *Digital Minimalism* by Cal Newport) are continuously being pumped into our social atmosphere—that we have not yet developed a healthy relationship with communication technologies in the twenty-first century. And we never really have.

For example, during the post-World War II economic boom, Television (TV) became one of the most notable communication technologies on the market. "Where there had been **only 178,000 televisions in homes in 1948**, by 1955, over **three-quarters of a million US households**—about half of all homes—had television".[41]

However, unlike modern digital technologies, the TV was a one-way street of information. A TV is a communication consumption technology, meaning people cannot interact with incoming information. And we already know how quickly TVs became addictive and socially isolating— "In 1949-1950, American households were already watching *4 hours and 35 minutes of TV per day*".[42]

When you throw a *two-way* communication technology into people's hands, what do you think happens to general populaces addictive tendencies toward technology abuse?

I won't make the claim that we need to banish all social media use or any communication technology, for that matter. As we discovered previously, revolutionizing technologies like social media, are extremely versatile and **can be used in both positive and negative ways**. The problem is, the current generational software installed into our Thoughtware is gravitating toward the negative spectrum.

For example, "One survey revealed that **74 percent of Millennials prefer conversing digitally rather than in person**. While this helps them communicate more efficiently, it diminishes their communication effectiveness".[43]

In being unable to communicate effectively when social media is used irresponsibly, it can lead us astray and amplify depression and anxiety as we discussed in Chapter 1. And as this trend becomes increasingly prevalent, we also find that it impacts another key component of our *Thoughtware*—**Attention.**

"Some studies suggest the rise of Attention Deficit Hyperactivity Disorder (ADHD) is **directly associated with overuse of social media**, as our brain easily loses focus due to ongoing demands for our attention".

In addition to our lack of focus prompted by social media use, we also know that throughout our maturation, we will inherently become less accepting and less friendly toward new ideas. Applying these concepts to the workplace, it seems rather apparent why people tend to live in a snapshot of the past—whether it be focusing on old data sets, as we saw with genetic sequencing, or pre-digital revolution education techniques, as we saw with education's attraction toward standardized tests and rote-learning.

Human Thoughtware is not built for the twenty-first century. Synthetic evolution has reached an exponential rate of change that's impossible to keep up with. However, we can still do something about it. Evolutionarily, humans are by far the most adaptable organism that we know of because of the unique components that construct our minds. Among these components, we will analyze four notable ones that make up this *Thoughtware* and how and when they dramatically change, both naturally and when we introduce powerful mind-altering substances like psychedelics.

1. **Environmental Software**—Situational/Changes over millions of years
2. **Genetic Software**—Inherited/Changes over hundreds of thousands of years
3. **Cultural Software**—Learned/Changes over centuries
4. **Generational Software**—Learned/Changes over decades

THE EVOLUTION OF THOUGHTWARE

Throughout the process of evolution, life has been experimenting and reformulating how to construct the best blueprint—a blueprint that loosely defines how to build an organism.

In the early nineteenth century, Charles Darwin became one of the first well-recognized explorers of this blueprint with his book "*On the Origin of Species*", published in 1859. Darwin proposed that an organism will take on different physical and mental forms gradually over the course of many successive generations.

This mechanism can be thought of as a *random* sacrificial procedure, which tests different variations of a species as they interact with the environment. The variations that became successful were those that lived long enough to reproduce. In other words, some natural process selects reproductively successful organisms—hence *natural selection*.[44]

If you want to build a concrete understanding of this idea, David Buss's book, *Evolutionary Psychology*, navigates through this selection process in more detail. For now, the important takeaway is that, by nature, the current classification of humans is only temporary.[45]

Seven years after Darwin published his book on natural selection, a scientist named Gregor Mendel published a book after tinkering around with pea plants. He discovered that life's blueprint is composed of small information molecules known as genes, in which the collection of all these genes makes up a vast library of information called a genome. For this reason, Mendel is still known as the "*father of modern genetics*". (Fun fact: the molecule that makes up these genes, DNA, wasn't discovered until nearly one hundred years later by James Watson in 1953.)

With both Darwin's and Mendel's contributions, our species realized that, like any great idea or product, the human genome spontaneously changes, testing various combinations of biological toolsets. With this instruction manual handy and the influence of natural selection, humans have grown both intellectually and physically to combat the environmental pressures they face. While these processes occur unconsciously to us, some level of thought still mandates them. And so, we arrive at the first two layers of human Thoughtware.

This first layer is the *environmental software*, which includes all behavioral influences that occur outside the human body. In other words, this environmental software is composed of all the external interactions that shape who we are—like climate, access to physiological necessities, or predatorial threats, among many others. This layer is highly situational because of the vast differences in ecosystems across the globe.

In response to this environmental software, the genes that create our bodies and our minds are then thrown into the evolutionary boxing ring. The genome sequence that creates the best biological tools for a given environment wins the fight. That's why animals in the jungle look completely different from those that live in the artic! The winner then finds a mating partner and produces offspring with a new variation of genes. This book will not go into the details about how this process works, but for now, we will refer to it as the second layer of Thoughtware, our *genetic software.* This software includes all the inherited behavioral influences that occur inside the human body.

With the present version of our genetic software, the human mind has built five different sensory tools, each designed to take in a different medium of information–*touch, smell, taste, sound,* and *sight.*

But the truly fascinating part about our mental hardware, which makes us stand out among all other species, is that it is equipped with software that can subjectively manipulate data at a high level.

Our sensory perception is **not limited by the amount of information in an environment.**

Rather, it is **limited by the number of symbols** a civilization uses to **represent information in an environment.**

With these two ideas, we can now describe the next two layers of our Thoughtware, *cultural software* and *generational software*. While generational software is a collection of modern symbols in a society, *cultural software* is a collection of both historical and modern symbols. In other words, a generation is simply an extension of a society's culture. It's the breath of lungs, the music of instruments, or more relevantly to this book, the mood-disorders of a society.

More specifically, Michael Winkelman, a neuro-theologist and medical anthropologist, states, *"As we grow up, [our] mental hardware is shaped and programmed by the cultural software that we acquire from the other members of our society"*.[46]

For example, we can see this cultural software in action by shedding some light on the objects around us, quite literally. The way we understand *color* is entirely guided by our cultural software, and some cultures use a completely different color schematic to make sense of their visual world.

W.H.R. Rivers, an English anthropologist of the late nineteenth century and early twentieth century, says color language correlates to a *"culture's general intellect and cultural development."* Reinforcing this idea, two other anthropologists, Brent Berlin and Paul Kay, examined the evolution of color language cross-culturally. When they traveled to the southwestern Pacific isles of Papua New Guinea and the tropical wetlands of the Philippines, they came to some interesting conclusions.

In Papua New Guinea, instead of utilizing an array of made-up words like blue or red to make sense of color, their culture developed an entirely different technique to understand light. In their native language, Yele, they took their color abstraction to a whole new level. They began identifying a broad range of objects that shared a similar color. For example, instead of calling something blue, they would use the sky to classify it as blue. Or instead of gray, it would be ash color.

In the Philippines, we see yet another set of rules to understand color. The Hanunoo people break down color into four different dimensions: wetness (*green*) versus dryness (*red*) and lightness (*white*) versus darkness (*black*). We can see how this system was derived based on the habitat of their culture. The wetness versus dryness of a color would refer to the hydration level of a crop, while the lightness versus darkness would refer to the degree of the hydration.[47]

For example, a member of this culture might see a wilting crop. They would note the dryness or wetness and the intensity of those color features using lighten or darkness. A *dark yellow-red* would indicate that the crop is suffering from severe dehydration or has already wilted away, whereas on the opposite spectrum, a *dark green*, would indicate that the plant is doing well. However, I'll leave the other color translations (*the colors inside the 'grey' area*), up to the professional botanists' deductions.

The key takeaway from these cultures is that colors are ways of symbolizing abstract information (*light*) from the environment. In this respect, we can see that colors are just one medium in which we can place subjective identities on information from the world, identities entirely mandated by culture. If I were to suddenly create my own nomenclature about a color, it wouldn't provide any communicatory value. However, I could instead integrate a wide range of colors onto one object, effectively making my own color hierarchy. I'd be using the same color language, but depending on how the colors are arranged, I could perhaps then call it Art instead of nonsense.

This helps us answer why six million people visit the Mona Lisa at the Louvre each year.[47] In other words, instead of *reinventing the color-wheel* of language, I would just be re-inventing the technique to create it as Leonardo did in his painting. The Mona Lisa is a rather small painting with dimensions of 30" x 21", but regardless of the physical quantity of information contained within the painting, it still touches the deepest depths of many individual's souls, inspiring them to tackle their artistic ambitions.

Transitioning back to the digital revolution era, the iPhone is still the most popular cellular device for this reason. It has a unique user interface, designed with this culture software in mind. Plenty of cellphones are much more computationally advanced, but, still, the iPhone holds the number-one spot for most popular.

Millions of humans are so infatuated with their cellular devices it because condenses insane amounts of information into little information packets called apps. The popular ones are culturally appropriated by a larger population of people.

This cultural component makes our communication abilities limitless because we can always create more symbols. However, this also eludes to why many people find it difficult to communicate in the twenty-first century. Creating symbols is a learned behavior, and as technology starts automating this process for us, not only will it start speaking for us as it already does with auto-correct technologies, but it will start understanding our own cultural software **better than we do**.

As more humans stop using the cognitive superpower that has allowed the human-animal to prosper up the evolutionary leader board, bad things start to happen.

The brain"is a garden and you have to irrigate it and stimulate and tend to all the corners, particularly ones you're starting to neglect. **Getting out of the box and engaging the recesses of your mind is the most important thing. Then, the creative things happen**", assures Rahul Jandial (author of Neuro Fitness and Neurosurgeon in Los Angeles).

Jandial adds, "If you're not using parts of it, it'll program itself to let those parts of the garden wither. So, **the diversity of thinking and the depth of thinking just one level past what you're used to is the way to keep the whole garden flourishing**".[48]

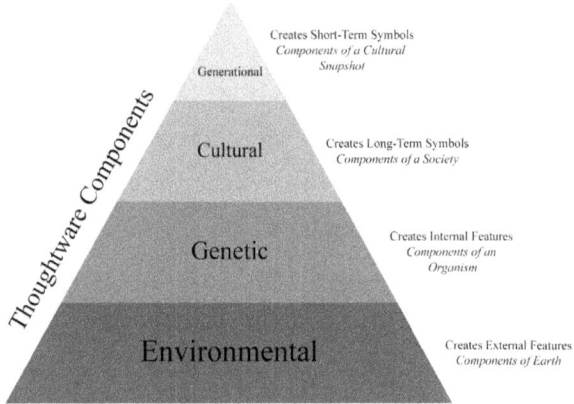

As we can see with the hierarchy of Thoughtware components, we could increase communication abilities by altering our genetics. However, if we ask whether our genes are changing as fast as technology, the answer is a resounding no based on Darwinian evolution.[49]

While modern gene-editing technologies like CRISPR-Cas9 are extremely promising for our future, I expect it won't be a technology used by the general public for many years to come, especially since there doesn't seem to be a clear ethical resolution about this topic no matter what country you go to. Just recently a Chinese researcher, He JianKui, was shackled up and condemned for "deliberately evading oversight" and creating the first gene-edited baby.[50]

The ethical boundaries surrounding gene editing in humans is still a fuzzy subject, not to mention humanity lacks a deeper understanding of human genetics in its entirety. Genetics is an extremely new field of scientific inquiry, so it's to be expected.

On the other hand, *I might sound like a broken record by now*, but people can reprogram their Thoughtware effectively in other ways, without the extreme costs of experimental gene-editing technologies or wasting hundreds of dollars on SSRI anti-depressants. While psychedelics don't specifically target our genetics, rest assured, they can briefly alter our neurochemistry, which is a component of our genetic software (it's in the same layer). In turn, this temporal mode of alteration can then cause a rippling effect (*the butterfly effect*), as we mentioned in Chapter 1, which slightly adjusts our cultural software and subsequently, our generational software.

So how do we do it?

First, we can deliberately focus our attention on cultural software and how it has changed over the last few centuries. By carefully and responsibly employing the use of these examples, we may find that psychedelics is the most passive and cognitively liberalizing tool that humans have access too.

CULTURAL SOFTWARE

We also find that culture is so deeply ingrained in the human species that it becomes especially problematic when new ideas rise to the surface of human thought. If an idea starts to make major changes to this cultural software, resistance is sure to follow. That's why there is always an underlying cultural influence about what ideas are communicated.

The more socially unaccepted an idea is, the more controversy arises. From an evolutionary perspective, humans tend to avoid controversy when they can in hopes of not being ostracized from a community. When isolated from the rest of the population, it becomes rather challenging to pass on offspring. So, it's imperative when voicing an interpretation, an opinion, that the mind's social value system, the culture, is in alignment with the rest of the population.

To take an extreme example, slavery is a cultural phenomenon, a social belief system that a large population desperately clung to. As cultural resistance to this idea became widespread, the very moral compass that allowed people to keep slaves started pointing in the opposite direction. It seems obvious now that slavery is bad. But sadly, this only a recent cultural perspective. India still has 18.4 million slaves, followed by China at 3.4 million and Pakistan at 2.1 million. Of the 195 recognized countries in the world, 167 countries still exercise slavery. That's nearly 86 percent of the countries in the world.[51]

Changing a cultural ideology, especially one rooted through-out many generations, is no easy task. However, "if at least 25 percent of a community's population is committed to chang-ing what is considered the social norm, the group will see a shift".[52] This shift then transpires through individuals within a community, updating their cultural software to account for the new perspective. However, if we look at the popula-tion of America, 25 percent is still an overwhelmingly large number—83 million people.

It's easy to point out that all of humanity's problems are culturally stimulated, but the challenge comes down to altering a perspective that has become platitudinous. This social framework is an enslaving beast that targets every-one. Science, engineering, business, education, and all other work disciplines are no exception. Each of these disciplines is composed of humans, fit with their own set of interpreta-tions and value systems. Even the way we present solutions to problems are colored with cultural biases. For example, climate change is largely influenced by the insistence of livestock as a food source. In 2017, nearly 42 percent of agricultural-related greenhouse gas emission (chemicals like carbon dioxide, methane and nitrous oxide that trap heat within Earth's atmosphere) comes from livestock producing methane gas.[53] Or on a larger scale, livestock and livestock-related activities (fertilizer use) **contributes to nearly 18 percent of all human-made greenhouse gas emissions** finds Henning Steinfeld, head of the livestock sector analysis in Rome, Italy.[54]

Simply telling a population to slow down their meat consumption is out of the question. America has developed a cultural attraction to meat, and trying to change this perspective borders on the difficulty of abolishing slavery if not more so. With the rise of civilization in 3000 BCE, Mesopotamia being the first known, slavery found its beginnings.[55] However, meat consumption for hominids like ourselves dates back nearly 2.6 million years ago.[56]

Humans have only loosely accepted the idea of eliminating slavery by rewiring an idea supplemented for over 5000 years. In America, it took almost one hundred years for enough cultural resistance to develop (launching the deadliest American war to date, the Civil War, with a death count around 800,000)[57] and remove labels associated with slaves. While slavery was finally relinquished in the post-war reconstruction era, it took America another one hundred years to successfully decouple ethnicity from human rights as a result of the Civil Rights Movement in the 1960s.

In proportion to abolishing slavery, it would take 52,000 years to abolish meat consumption and who knows how many lives lost. By that point, climate change would already have extinguished all land-based organic life. Clearly, taking the same violent approach when abolishing slavery is not applicable when abolishing meat consumption.

Before the question, *"what's the right approach to solve these cultural problems?"*, pops into the mind—as a reminder, this book's objective is not to propose some novel methodology to tackle a specific problem. Instead, if we realize that these problems are artificially created, self-installed over continual generational succession, we can elucidate the fundamental pieces of our **cultural software**. And if our goal is to uninstall it's more primitive aspects (like keeping slaves), our approach to solve these various problems is to target the Thoughtware itself and update it with a bit of psychedelic intervention.

THOUGHTWARE UPDATE

In order to achieve a Thoughtware update (a Mind Leap) the first thing we must understand, before addressing psychedelic induced versions of Thoughtware, is its typical circuitry on a conceptual level.

In other words, how does information flow through typical human Thoughtware?

To answer this question, we will break it down into four components we've briefly discussed—Environment, Interpretation, Culture, and Knowledge.

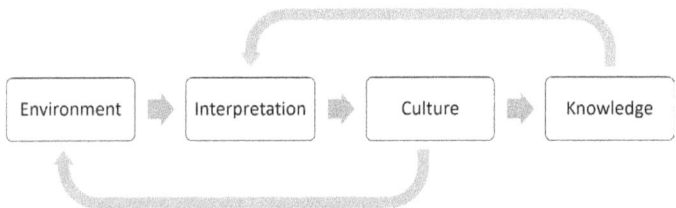

A conceptual flowchart detailing the flow of information in human Thoughtware.

The *environment* serves as the baseline for developing our interpretations of the world. All the stimuli that surround a population of people, including its vegetation, biodiversity, and climate, among many others, form the basis for this sector. *Interpretation* then enters the mix when we actively choose to observe said stimuli and construct opinions about each. After consultation among others in a population, the *accepted interpretations* of the world then build the **foundations of a *culture*.** For example, if someone declared slaves are bad, it would only become accepted as a component of the culture if that idea was mutually agreed upon.

Finally, the people within a culture decide whether an accepted interpretation is *truly accurate*. The accuracy of an interpretation, or how well an idea describes some natural phenomena, is then tested against a few other alternative descriptions. The chosen descriptor becomes cultural **knowledge**. The idea slaves are bad only becomes knowledge when a culture decides that keeping slaves is detrimental to its long-term prosperity.

The interesting thing is that *knowledge is not an absolute*. It can change because the starting line, the environment, is not a static system. As a culture accumulates knowledge of the world, the ways we interpret it also change. For example, the claim that the sun revolves around the earth, the geocentric model, became a social norm. We can see this idea resonating among many religious texts and its subsequent influence on culture.

For example, the Bible Chronicles 16:30 and Psalm 104:5 prophesizes, "Tremble before [God], all the earth! The **world is firmly established; it cannot be moved**" read Chronicles 16:30. In Psalm 104:5, this concept is pushed further, reading "[God] established the earth upon its foundations, so that it will **not totter forever and ever.**"

In turn, these quotes magnify **culturally hard-wired** beliefs defining earth as an **unmovable** and **unwavering** land mass. With this perspective, Earth was portrayed as the center of the universe, a landmass of divine intervention from which all transpires from. Furthermore, as the bible, among many other religious texts, electrified human Thoughtware and manifested within their cultural software, most innovative models about the true nature of Earth's motion withered away in the face of mass cultural resistance.

Only after the invention of the telescope and Galileo's work in astronomy and planetary orbiting was this concept finally disproven. However, his heliocentric model, which portrayed the earth revolving around the sun (debunking religious beliefs embracing the geocentric model), had yet to be accuracy tested. It was still but a loose concept accepted by a few members of tightly knit scientific culture when Nicolaus Copernicus published his work in 1543 about the heliocentric model. It took over 70 years for this idea to be proven and another 150 for it to become appropriated into cultural knowledge. Humanity then started building their interpretations of the world not based on earth being the center of the universe, but a fragment of dust following gravity's natural order.

With this in mind, we can see that an accepted interpretation of the world has a gestation period. It takes time for it to work its way through the ranks of culture. Think of it like riding a bike. In the beginning, training wheels are attached to the bike until its user becomes comfortable balancing without them. After a bit of testing and a few scraped knees, the user starts to become confident in his abilities without the training wheels.

In much the same way, an idea must go through the same process. Initially, an interpretation becomes accepted—the idea is granted permission to start using training wheels. This accepted interpretation then starts to make its way throughout the entire culture supplemented by these training wheels. Only after becoming confident in the idea are the training wheels removed and a culture is left to decide whether that idea should become knowledge. Often, however, just one bike is not granted training wheels. Or in the case of proving the heliocentric model, a model already exists without training wheels. For the incoming interpretation to prevail, it must be faster and more balanced than the opposing one. Disproving the geocentric model became challenging because it had existed without training wheels for so long among many other political and religious reasons against the heliocentric model.

The last component of the flow chart model is the most dangerous aspect of human culture. With enough cultural motivation, humanity can alter the very fabric of the environment.

Pollution and over-consumption of earth's natural resources can dramatically influence the world we live in and the longevity of those that live in it. Again, pointing this out doesn't really help us solve the problem. Cleaning up trash on the beaches or limiting your waste production are good things. But still, these good deeds are just temporary treatments to the symptoms that arise from a culture motivated to consume more, produce more, and grow exponentially.

It takes centuries to change a cultural climate, and it becomes rather challenging to identify what idea might transpire effectively through a culture. The cultural software we have become so attached to is in dire need of an update. Luckily, there's one more dimension to the model proposed above. The human mind can operate at more than just one state of interpretation.

Rather, with a careful blend of internal manipulation, in our *genetic software layer*, the interpretive mode of the mind can be altered, changing our *cultural software*, to focus in on specific sets of problems, mandated by our *generational software*. In other words, by engaging a psychedelic version of Thoughtware, we can experience reality in multiple different facets. And as we found out in Chapter 2, we can approach each version of reality (generated by our *Thoughtware*) at a neurochemical level. In doing this, we form the basis for which many individuals can update their Thoughtware and break past our own attachments to outdated beliefs about reality.

PART II

PSYCHEDELIC WAVES

As we've begun to wrap our minds around the potential for psychedelics, it's important to keep this idea in mind because it seems we've forgotten about the ways in which our curiosity toward psychedelics and our subsequent consumption has supplemented humanity's unique talents to innovate and master both the **material** and the **spiritual world**.

Sadly, it seems many of the valuable insights brought on by our first encounters with psychedelics have been lost during the scuffle of the 1960s. Psychedelics are by no stretch of the imagination *new*. For humans, they are age-old devices, with the first documented use being nearly 9,000 years ago. This first interaction sparked the *first wave* of the psychedelic revolution. In this Chapter of hominid existence, psychedelic consumption was something special, ceremonial, and well-nourished by early tribal communities looking to embrace their proximity to spiritual divinity.

However, as more members of the human species gained awareness about these substances through popularization during America's counterculture rebellion, the *second wave*, their roaring flames of potential became extinguished for a large majority. But the validity of decades of mass media programming has started to change in the modern era. As more psychedelic research facilities, like the Multidisciplinary Association for Psychedelic Studies (*MAPS*), The Heffter Research Institute (*HRI*), and John Hopkins Center for Psychedelic and Consciousness Research (*JHCP*), spring up from the smoldering flames of the second wave, more and more negative claims made about psychedelics during the second wave are starting to return **false positives**.

With scientific research developing a firm backbone in which we can reconceptualize these chemicals on a global scale, in 2019, we have now entered the Third Wave of the Psychedelic Revolution.

In Part II–Psychedelic Waves, we will go on a psychedelic roller coaster ride, exploring the peaks and troughs of each wave and collecting valuable insights that were left behind. As we approach the third wave, we might just see how psychedelics can enable a *Mind Leap*.

CHAPTER 4

STONED APE
HYPOTHESIS

———

"Psilocybes gave our hominid ancestors 'access to realms of supernatural 'power,' 'catalyzed the emergence of human self-'reflection,' and 'brought us out of the animal mind and into the world of articulated speech and imagination.'

This last hypothesis about the invention of language turns on the concept of synesthesia, the conflation of the senses that psychedelics are known to induce: under the influence of psilocybin, numbers can take on colors, colors attach to sounds, and so on.

Language, [Terence McKenna] contends, represents a special case of synesthesia, in which otherwise meaningless sounds become linked to concepts. Hence, the stoned ape: by giving us the gifts of language and self-reflection psilocybin mushrooms made us who we are, transforming our primate ancestors into Homo sapiens".[58]

While Mckenna's *Stoned Ape Hypothesis* that claims psilocybin mushrooms transformed our primate ancestors into Homo sapiens *(as recounted in Pollan's book)* seems a bit far-fetched, there might be some truth to his hypothesis. As we set the stage for *Altered Minds* in Part I, we found that scientists like Hagen and Sullivan found *long-term evolutionary* relationships between humans and psychotropic drugs. And we also know that these substances can permanently change a person's personality after just one psychedelic experience with psilocybin mushrooms.

When we combine these two ideas together and then mix in the one element that distinguishes the human-animal from other species—culture—the resulting cocktail of ideas might resemble Mckenna's conclusion. That is, the defining feature that has led to humanity's rapid adaptation and subsequent conquest over the material world is due to our desire to cooperate within a medium where abstract symbols collide, forming the basis for the *cultural software* we discussed previously.

This level of the hierarchy of our *Thoughtware* makes humans so exceptional at communicating among themselves, and yet the curious question is why are humans the only ones who've developed such complex cultural software, or with Pollan's idea cocktail in mind, what transformed *the stoned ape's* cultural software into the modern *homo sapien* one?

In other words, how did *the stoned ape* achieve a *Mind Leap?*

While the exact biochemical changes that allowed this transition to take place might remain a mystery, if we hone our attention to our *environmental software*, a component embedded in all organisms since life itself is constantly interacting with the world, we realize humans are the only species capable of using *advanced* technologies. And by *advanced* technologies, I'm not talking about sticks and stones, which modern apes do use while foraging. I'm talking about technologies that use *multiple components of the environment* and brew them together into an inseparable, synthetic tool, non-existent throughout terrestrial history.

Wheels and *boats* are advanced technologies, whereas sticks and stones are *primitive* technologies. Wheels and boats are tools transformed from sticks—glued or carved together in such a way that the materials used to create them are *forever changed.*

For this reason, psychedelics may have been the first *advanced technology* humans used, most likely by coincidence. You might initially think this doesn't make sense. Mushrooms like the fly amanita (*amanita muscaria*), distinguished by a red cap speckled with white dots, naturally produce the main psychoactive ingredient in psychedelics, psilocybin—just like trees that naturally shed useful sticks.

However, what makes these psychedelic compounds advanced instead of primitive technologies, is not because using the drug in isolation has value, but rather, when we **consume** it, a neurological cocktail is *brewed* in the brain, deriving a new tool—an **altered state of consciousness (*ASC*)**. In other words, two products from the environment, psilocybin and human's unique neurochemistry, are mixed together, creating an *advanced* technology unavailable to other species.

For example, another animal that actively seeks these hallucinogenic mushrooms is reindeer. But when reindeer consume these mushrooms, they behave "in a *drunken fashion, running about aimlessly* and *making strange noises.* Head-twitching is also common."

In addition, while reindeer can break down the toxic substances contained within mushrooms, "the main psychoactive constituents remain unmetabolized and are excreted in the urine."

Or when we visit the South America rain forests, we've filmed "jaguars behaving in a *kittenish manner* after gnawing the bitter roots and bark of yage *(Banisteriopsis caapi)*,or more commonly—ayahuasca, containing the active psychedelic DMT, which is "a hallucinogenic vine that is also used by native tribes in ritualistic ceremonies. Some anthropologists believe that man first learned to use the drug after watching jaguars".[59]

Outside of mammalian species like reindeer and jaguars, we also observe interesting behavioral effects when psychedelics are introduced into arachnids. For example, in 1971, Peter N. Witt, a researcher at the North Carolina Department of Mental Health, continued the twenty-two-year-long investigation of spider-web-building and its sensitivity to drugs by giving spiders drugs—most relevantly LSD, among a large list of other chemicals like Adderall, sugar water, and Valium.

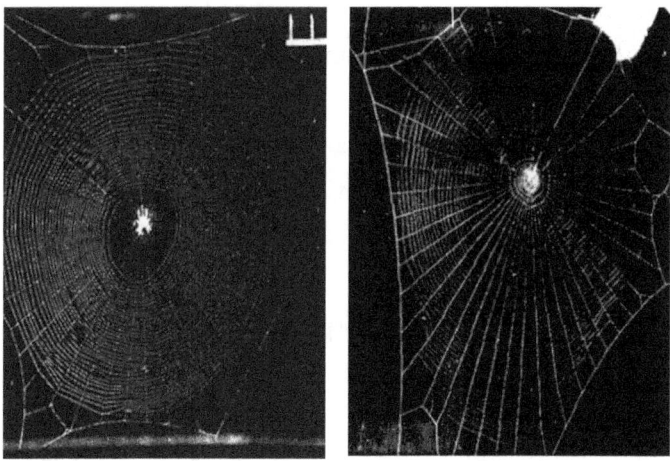

*Left—**control web** without the influence of drugs. **Right—LSD web** twelve hours after consuming less than 0.05ug LSD-25 by mouth in sugar water.* (Drugs Alter Web-Building of Spiders, Witt 1971)

What's fascinating about this study is that, while under the influence of LSD, at high doses, greater than 0.05ug of LSD-25, spider webs became rather irregular and ineffective. However, "Witt reported that spiders that had received less than 0.05ug, built webs of *larger than control size*, with *fewer oversized angles* and *significantly more-regular central angles* than in webs built the day before".[60]

In other words, at the right chemical dosage, Witt discovered that spiders create more effective spider webs in comparison to the *sober*, control webs. Among all other chemicals Witt tested, LSD, *structurally like the chemicals psilocybin and DMT*, was the only drug that "resulted in *unusually regular webs*".

However, while we can search through the vast catalog of all the interactions each animal has with psychedelics, it's quite clear that their effects are vastly different among species. Psilocybin unleashes a mental rampage inside the reindeer, DMT sedates jaguars as they embrace their *kittenish* play-fulness, and micro amounts of LSD allow spiders to weave more regular and larger web-structures. As we widen our scope to many other types of species, we also find that "*there is strong evidence that chimpanzees, baboons, monkeys, cats, dogs, and other animals hallucinate [suggesting] that altered states of consciousness and hallucinations are a function of the mammalian, not just the human, nervous system,*" as stated by lead archeologist research, J. D. Lewis-Williams.[61]

But when early hominids ingested psychedelics, we find something even more interesting about the resulting **ASC** (altered state of consciousness) that pushed our early ancestors to undergo a Mind Leap. Unlike other organisms, psychedelics transformed our minds into something with incredible utility, a powerful *advanced* technology that constructed the foundations for humans' complex communication abilities—or so the *Stoned Ape Hypothesis* suggests.

But what's the truth behind such a hypothesis?

Why did people like Mckenna, among the countless other archaeologists and anthropologists, think psychedelics were essential ingredients to humanity's cognitive prowess?

PAINTING WITH DUNG

As we journey back into the earliest documented era of Homo sapiens cognitive road map, few mediums exist in which we can really analyze psychedelic's historical presence. The year is 9000 BCE and humans have just entered the last stages of the "Stone Age",(*the Upper Palaeolithic Era*). Complex agricultural systems lie in the wake of human imagination, invented around 8000 BCE, and the first human civilization in 5000 BCE, Mesopotamia, still lives in the abyssal depths of the unknown. Furthermore, all forms of information storage outside of human biology have yet to be discovered, with cuneiform, a form of writing chiseled on stones, not appearing until 3000 BCE.[62]

Yet we can still visit two more avenues that might provide us with insights about psychedelics' effects throughout early hominid history, *cave paintings*—staples in nearly every anthropology and history textbook known to modern man and, *animal droppings*—nutrient-rich deposits from which fungi, like the fly amanita, would feast on to grow their vast fungal empire.

By observing specific elements of *cave paintings* and analyzing the migration patterns of animals in which droppings were sprinkled along the way, we can pinpoint regions across the globe of localized artistry (with paintings) and, likely, the major motivating force for early hominid's geographic expansion and developing imagination (animal dung containing psilocybin mushrooms).

MIMICRY AND FANTASY

But my curiosity with these paintings is not about the inks and dyes they used or how these paintings describe what they saw. No, my curiosity is about the entities they painted that did not exist. In other words—paintings that were not **mimicking reality**, like those that depict buffaloes or other humans, but paintings that were **recounting fantasies** that lived within their minds.

These paintings are important to our adventure through the first wave of psychedelics because they represent the **earliest** pieces of evidence underlying human's ability to communicate the imaginary – the components that shape human identity and perspective. While cave paintings themselves are historical artifacts, the **behavior** that led ancestral societies to splatter colors on cave walls is still a staple in human culture.

For example, as cave paintings became relics over thousands of years, clothing fashion replaced them and became the dominant cultural medium to communicate the imaginary. Today, when people choose to wear a custom suit or casual t-shirt, a decorated dress or mini-skirt or a shiny watch or pair of earrings, it's easy to forget that a deeper phenomenon (similar to the one that early cave painters experienced) underlies their decision-making process. More specifically, fashion-choice acts as a **symbolic form of self-representation**.

In some cultures, professional attire (suits and dresses) communicates the desire to look **put-together**, while casual attire (shirts and skirts) — the desire to look **relaxed**. And of course, the list goes on for many various fashion choices in different cultures.

In other words, fashion is just another facet of a culture that helps people solidify and communicate their identities at a given point in time. In this sense, symbolic cave paintings accomplish a very similar objective; The only difference is that cave paintings dress cave walls while clothes dress human bodies. But the fascinating aspect regardless of what we're choosing to stylize, the fundamental question is why are humans the only creatures built with artistic capacities?

What early human activities launched the emergence of symbolic communication, and subsequently, more complex imaginary ideas like fashion or on larger scale, written language and money?

When was humanity's first **Mind Leap**?

This is where cave paintings start to become a crucial element to support modern speculation. Across the globe, archaeologists are finding significant reasons to believe that ASCs may have served as the primary fuel source to ignite the explosion behind human's artistic expression on cave walls. In other words, sometime during the transition from the "Stone Age" and into the "Agricultural Age", symbolic (imaginary) forms of cave art arose—those which used *"points, vertical lines, circles and zig-zags"*(*aniconic graphemes*) together with depictions of gods that have taken animal form (*zoomorphic images*).[63]

From the sandy metropolis of the Saharan desert, across the Atlantic and into the South African Amazonian Basin, and into the vast expanse of North America and the isle of Scandinavia, Archeologists have found significant reasons to believe that much of the inspiration embedded within cave paintings comes from hallucinatory states, *including those achieved through psychedelic consumption.*

But before we jump to conclusions and make the logical leap that all symbolic cave paintings and forms of expression were stimulated by psychoactive drugs, it's important to note that humans are capable of manifesting hallucinatory states without any outside influence. For example, *"fatigue, sensory deprivation, intense concentration, auditory driving, migraine, schizophrenia, hyperventilation, and rhythmic movement are some other generating factors".*[64] However, what's fascinating about these different ASCs, and for the same reason people call a handful of patterns *(aka symbols)*, psychedelic, is that each stimulates the human visual system in a specific way.

In other words, when the human mind is thrust into a hallucinatory state, an ASC, the human brain starts to interpret the world differently. The Thoughtware that arises from our environment and genetic software starts processing information in novel ways, giving rise to abstract geometries.

Back in the 1920s, when German American psychologist Heinrich Klüver popped peyote buttons with his lab assistant in the laboratory, he was one of the first scientists to start categorizing these psychedelic-induced hallucinations. Notably, he found four distinct groups, which he called *form constants,* such as tunnels and funnels, spirals, lattices including honey-combs and triangles, and cobwebs. But unaided by modern computational technologies, it was challenging to communicate this visual phenomenon.

However, in 2002, researchers conducted a study building off Klüver's initial ideas, publishing a paper called *"What Geometric Visual Hallucinations Tell Us about the Visual Cortex"*. What they found only reinforced the research done in the 1920s. Aided by computers, they modeled the geometric visual hallucinations of subjects after taking hallucinogens like LSD, cannabis, mescaline, or psilocybin. By studying how the human eye's retina, the component that sends light information to the brain, changes during ASCs, they generated these images.

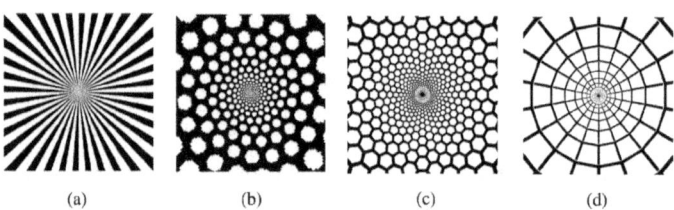

Hallucinatory form constants. (a) Funnel and (b) spiral images seen following inges-tion of LSD (c) honeycomb generated by marijuana, and (d) cobweb petroglyph

In other words, when we start observing cave paintings, we can identify, *with a high level of confidence*, that each halluci-natory state has a *hallucinatory form constant*, a reoccurring geometric structure, indicative of specific psychedelic drugs. When we hone our attention back to the ancestral era, it's interesting to see that we've been modeling, or in this era, painting these symbols for thousands of years.

ENTOPTIC PHENOMENA		SAN ROCK ART		COSO	PALAEOLITHIC ART			
		ENGRAVINGS	PAINTINGS		MOBILE ART		PARIETAL ART	
A	B	C	D	E	F	G	H	I
I								
II								
III								
IV								
V								
VI								

Image depicting symbolic forms of cave paintings, categorized by region and time period.

While the fidelity of claims supporting Mckenna's hypothesis,(*that psilocybin, among other psychedelics, primarily caused humans mental expansion*) is well-rooted within the modern scientific community, as we sift through the vast array of symbolic rock engravings and dig up research discussing hallucinogenic-induced geometries (*hallucinatory forms*), one of two important conclusions arise.

1. Psychotropic-ASCs have definitive impacts on humans' visual perception of the world.

And we compound this idea with cave paintings that more vividly describe their presence in early human societies like the following—

Cave paintings and incisions of prehistoric periods—during pre-literate history of human cultures. Left image depicts dancers holding mushroom-like objects found in the Tin-Tazarift rock art site at Tassil. Right image depicts masked figure with mushrooms sprouting from the fore-arms and thighs.[65]

It becomes rather easy to identify the second conclusion, as this image clearly depicts mushroom shapes—that is:

2. Psychotropics were well-embedded within humanity's ancestral societies.

However, these two ideas are not challenging to grapple with; rather, the magnitude of psychedelics significance really plagues the scientific community.

We draw the first two conclusions from modern scientific literature; however, Mckenna's hypothesis starts to press the hot buttons of the scientific community when he expands these conclusions by stating that the **primary reason the brain doubled in size** between the emergence of *Homo erectus* 1.8 million years ago and early Homo sapiens is **due to psychedelics.**

In other words, his suggestion is not that psychedelics **suddenly** catapulted Homo sapiens into evolving a type of cultural software capable of inventing symbolic technologies, like language and writing, in just a few millennia. We could falsify a claim like this rather quickly because, from Darwin's conjectures (*well-accepted by modern science*), humans' genetic software takes hundreds of thousands of years to be reprogrammed. To significantly alter the components of the human body, *by doubling the size of the brain*, is a feat that takes much more time than just a few thousand years.

However, Mckenna does suggest that psychedelics have been a part of human history since the dawn of the first hominid species, in which consumption of substances like psilocybin occurred over millions of years, giving rise to modern man's complex neurology gradually. With each subsequent generation of hominids, those that wielded psychedelics were the ones selected by nature to continue the vast future lineage of humanity.

At this point, animal droppings become a crucial element to Mckenna's hypothesis. At the same time, humans launched their hunter-gatherer careers 1.8 million years ago, animal tracking became an essential component of the hominid lifestyle. Following the trails of herding buffalo and other wild game by observing footprints and the dung they left behind was the essential ingredient of daily life. The interesting thing is that some of the dung they found most likely became birthing grounds for a wide variety of psilocybe mushrooms.

A NEEDLE IN THE HAYSTACK

"As primates descended from the forest canopies, went across the savanna, and [were] tracking animal's ungulates, what do [they] look for?

[They] look for footprints, paw prints, scat" (animal droppings")—*"the majority of primates are grub eaters"* (grubs burrow in scat). Paul Stamets, a well-known psilocybin enthusiast, continues, they *"run into the largest psilocybin mushroom in the world, growing bodaciously out of the dung of the animals [they're] tracking.*

They're hungry, it looks edible.

They ingest it."

Suddenly, *"they're catapulted into this incredible psychedelic experience—fractal patterns, mosaics, love, empathy—that doesn't happen once, that doesn't happen twice, that happens millions upon millions of times over hundreds and hundreds of thousands of years".*[66]

In 2017, Stamets made this claim supporting Mckenna's Stoned Ape Hypothesis at the annual Psychedelic Science

Conference, published by MAPS, igniting the flames of the underground psychedelic community, who've tucked this hypothesis away for decades. However, taken out of context and cut away from a thirty-three-minute-long lecture, filled to the brim with relevant scientific citations, soundbites like this creep their way into human imagination—not human literality.

Suggesting that fungi contained within dung was like finding a needle in the haystack of cognitive prosperity and cultural complexity still seems ridiculous to most individuals sucked away in their own tightly knit communities—communities that outwardly shy away from the investigations about the effects of these substances and humans biological relationship with them. Even if Mckenna, Stamets, and dozens of anthropologists, archaeologists, and neuroscientists make compelling arguments about psychedelics' potential to induce a *Mind Leap*, both ancestrally and presently, until we get passed the next bump on the psychedelic roller coaster, *the second wave*, it might be hard to consider these ideas with an open mind.

After all, we're talking about illegal, highly restricted schedule I substances in America—outlawed all throughout the European Union. There must be a rational reason behind psychedelics imprisonment.

Right?

CHAPTER 5

DOORS OF DECEIT

———

The *second wave* of the psychedelic revolution is not as won-derous or speculative as the *first wave*. It's an era of homo-sa-pien coercion, a period of enforcement, filled to the brim with hyper-competitive economic and territorial conquest. Thoughts of globalized cooperation were replaced with nationalized competition. Humans' newly found ability to exercise empathy or compassion was thrown to the wolves and, along with it, psychedelics.

Instead, the desire for fame, fortune, and control became one of the most powerful motifs boiling within the hearts of man. Over the course of several thousand years, after the birth of complex agriculture and the rise of civiliza-tion and language, this motif made a significant dent in human Thoughtware.

While many modern psychedelic enthusiasts might assume that the second wave begins with the counter-culture movement of America in the 1960s, it's important to understand that it was just the end of a long onslaught of psychedelic suppression. After the development of complex agricultural systems and turbulent civilizations, the thousands of years following the transition from the Stone Age into the Bronze Age in 3,000 BCE brought about great artistry and craftsmanship, technology and invention, and self-discovery and self-actualization.

However, as humanity's nomadic tendencies sprinkled communities across the world, the distance from psychedelic plants and fungi became greater and greater. As each community started gaining regional stability with their newfound invention of agriculture, many humans were reprogrammed to seek settlement, trading in their bow and arrow as proud hunters for field hoes and plows as desperate peasants. This was the Neolithic Era—initiated by The Agricultural Revolution.

THE AGRICULTURAL REVOLUTION

While agriculture allowed humanity to grow small societies into civilizations like Mesopotamia, in the modern era, it has been the subject of much controversy. Many historians argue it propelled humanity into an era of prosperity and innovation, while others proclaim it shackled us into eternal damnation. But we can draw one conclusion from this time period, which might help us discover why psychedelics became relics of the past inside civilizations.

As hunters and foragers turned into farmers and peasants, people stopped tracking animal footprints, littered with trails of magic mushrooms. Dense vegetation filled with a variety of different psychotropics like DMT and Ibogaine, native to South America and Africa, respectively, was no longer part of the territory called home. For ancient hunter-gatherers, Yuval Harari writes:

"Home was the entire territory, with its hills, streams, woods and open sky.

Peasants, on the other hand, spent most their days working a small field or orchard, and their domestic lives centered on a cramped structure of wood, stone, or mud, measuring no more than a few dozen feet—the house.

The typical peasant developed a very strong attachment to this structure, whose impact was psychological as much as architectural. Hence-forth, attachment to 'my house' and separation from the neighbors became the psychological hallmark of a much more self-centered creature."

In other words, with territorial attachment now erected in the confines of human Thoughtware, humanity's environmental software morphed from a migratory culture to one prioritizing settlement. The malleable putty of thoughts that allowed hunter-gatherers to adapt to a wide variety of habitats became a rigid metal, in which farmers and peasants were imprisoned by their home, locked into a single habitat, filled with constant worry about their plots of land.

With this in mind, we can answer two questions:

1. Why has the Agricultural Revolution been the subject of much controversy in the modern era?

2. How did the Agricultural Revolution spark the beginnings of the psychedelic's *second wave?*

AGRARIAN PHILOSOPHY

To answer the first question, agricultural revolution optimists might argue that this revolution brought great advancement in society, allowing technology and food to become more accessible, to grow and elevate civilization and the human population. Complex job markets, in which diverse skills were prioritized, allowed humanity to flourish with the influx of resources and tools. In effect, architectural artistry was no longer restricted by the impermanence of territory or lack of building materials—stimulating the birth of careers like engineering, fabric, and metalworking, among a large list of revolutionizing disciplines.

On the other hand, taking a pessimistic approach, we find that this caused rippling effects up the hierarchy of humans' Thoughtware, forging new genetic software from the agricultural diet of corn, rice, and wheat. As a result, humans' cultural software transformed—open plains became restricted by property deeds, in which farmers and peasants, the primary career path of agrarian-based societies, became infatuated with a desire to possess more fertile lands—to produce and sell more crops. This pessimistic interpretation serves as the basis for which these humans became much more 'self-centered creature(s).'

Most notably, power, violence, and control, hardwired components of humans' genetic software intended for defense, were modified for aggression to prevent trespassers from stealing their hard-earned plot of land or credit for ideas. Now, I won't make the claim that the agricultural revolution was the sole reason for human violence.

Inter-species violence was a commonality among early tribes as they sought ways to maximize food resources and survivability on their migratory journeys; however, organized violence at larger scales had yet to awaken—early hominids, the nomadic hunter-gatherer, had no need to defend specific territories and risk losing the lives and support of their best hunters and gatherers.

However, with humans' new cultural software, Joshua Mark, the chief editor of Ancient History Encyclopedia, writes, "The possession of permanent territories, to defend or conquer, brought the need for large-scale battle in which the losing army would be destroyed, the better to secure the disputed territory. The coming of 'civilization' therefore brought the need for organized bodies of shock troops".[67]

In this sense, human exploration, both territorially and mentally, became a mechanism to increase social status and economic prosperity. The desire to explore was fueled by thoughts soaked in power and currency, not survivability and curiosity. Warfare and military tactics were soon programmed into many humans' cultural software as the taste of blood delighted those who partook in humanity's first war in Mesopotamia in 2700 BCE. As warfare raged on for the next several centuries, social inequality spread faster than wildfires with the construction of social class systems and the employment of slavery.

While the optimistic historian might use this information by saying that this *inspired hyper-competition and therefore motivated people to climb the class hierarchy through innovation,* on the other hand, the pessimist would insist that this *dissolved humans ability to cooperate effectively, damaging two components of humans cultural software, empathy, and compassion, by trading them in for ruthlessness and selfishness.*

We might infer the optimist favors productive, while the pessimist—equality. Spoiler alert—the desire for productivity won, and from this psychological genocide of empathy and compassion, the fires of inequality grew brighter. However, this proved problematic for these ancient civilizations as political resistance against the rising inequality gap started developing into rebellions. Therefore, adds Joshua Mark, "Mesopotamia [was] a chronicle of nearly *constant strife*. Even after Sargon the Great of Akkad (2334-2279 BCE) unified the region under the Akkadian Empire, war was still waged in putting down rebellions."

However, throughout these several thousand years of civilizational development, a new program for humans' cultural software became the subject of much attention—religion.

To quiet political resistance, *imagined orders*, belief systems, served as the basis for the many ancient governing systems—AKA: *Theocracies*. For those at the top of the power hierarchy, this became an extremely valuable program to install into the lower social class's Thoughtware to prevent the onset of a revolution. Harari illustrates this installation protocol writing:

"How do you cause people to believe in an imagined order such as Christianity, democracy or capitalism? First, you never admit that the order is imagined. You always insist that the order sustaining society is an objective reality created by the great gods or by the laws of nature. People are unequal, not because Hammurabi said so, but because

Enlil and Marduk decreed it. People are equal, not because Thomas Jefferson said so, but because God created them that way. Free markets are the best economic system, not because Adam Smith said so, but because these are the immutable laws of nature."

With Harari's words in mind, the beauty of an imagined order is that, after a successful installation, suddenly control no longer needed to be enforced by human eyes. In other words, order that silenced internal rebellions with shiny blades, **a materialistic order**, was much less effective than with a Thoughtware program, **an imagined order**.

This is because an imagine order works on its own accord, using the eyes of God or nature to mandate the human-animal's behavioral functions. For example, in the ancient civilization, The Shang Dynasty founded around 1600 BCE, its founder, T'ang the Completer, would announce to his people, *"God has given to every man a conscience; and if all men **acted in accordance with its dictates**, they would not stray from the right path. The way of God is to **bless the good** and **punish the bad**. He has sent down calamities on the House of Hsia, to make manifest its crimes".*[68]

These phrases, *bless the good* and *punish the bad*, are the key to understanding how this imagined order works. Good and bad are mandated by the governing body; however, by enforcing that good and bad are really objects created by *God*, the government can enforce unjustified mandates within a society, calling on God as a scapegoat when resistance starts to form. When questioned, rulers might say, "This is all God's doing, we're just the messengers."

So, when we throw all these variables into one cultural soup, at some point, the controversy that arises from this period comes down to taste—in which optimists might think an imagined order is an essential ingredient for creating cooperative civilizations, while pessimists might think this ingredient is just a way of masking the tormenting taste of inequality. Surely, this debate will continue for many generations.

Regardless of the side we align with, by highlighting how human Thoughtware changed over this era, from migratory to domesticated species and from materialistic to imaginary governing, these factors help shape the answer to the second question we proposed.

CULTURAL MALWARE VERSION 1.0

With humans now locked into specific regions, there was no escaping the imagined order. While it might seem like I'm referring to an 'imagined order' as this terrible thing that has only harmed humanity, that's just not true—like all other technologies, whether it's a cultural software program like religion or psychedelic-induced ASCs, they all have the potential for abuse.

Religion is an extremely powerful tool, and many studies have found compelling relationships between religious participation and lower morbidity and mortality rates for virtually all diseases.[69] However, religions used in ancient civilization walk a narrow tightrope, in which mediating human behavior *healthily* is drastically depended on restrictive factors like diet, drug use, and sex.[70]

And this is exactly where the problem lies. When more *self-centered creatures* start navigating their way to the top of the power hierarchy, there's a high chance they start abusing the religious control switch, turning all the knobs and pressing all the buttons to ensure individualistic, not communal, prosperity.

For example, with the rise of Mesopotamia, bartering, trading goods like grain and cattle for other necessities, was slowly replaced by another imagined order—**money**. However, money was still in its infantile stages—the idea that the value of an entity was instilled by a culture and not the object itself, wasn't a very attractive idea. How could someone trust in an object with no inherent value?

Livestock could be used for food and leather, while a lump of money had no direct utility. However, as we transcended into the Iron Age in 1200 BCE, money became defined by weight in gold or silver, and with this new metric in place, humans didn't have to worry that their money would depreciate—the weight of precious metals, melted down into small chips called coins, carried its own sense of cultural trust.

When the 'first official' currency was minted in Lydia in 600 BCE, suddenly the greed simmering in our minds manifested to a boil. With this imagined order well-programmed into many humans' Thoughtware, the search for gold and treasure became a staple throughout the thirteenth to the sixteenth century, forming the basis for the first globalized *cultural malware*—a type of software that places emphasis on two components (1) **control and** (2) **greed,** instead of empathy and generosity.[71]

For example, when Spanish conquistadors like Hernán Cortés and Francisco Pizarro led the European charge to sequester their greed, this cultural malware developed psychedelic's second wave into a more rigid shape. As they sailed across the bumpy waves of the Atlantic Ocean, landing on the rocky shores of the Yucatan Peninsula in Mexico in 1519, treasure was one of the only things on their mind. Upon arriving (*at what is now called Mesoamerica*), this cultural malware dug deep roots within the landscape—launching one of the first large-scale culture shocks against psychedelics.

WAVES OF PROHIBITION

In Mesoamerica, the Aztec civilization was the largest cultural hub, in which psychedelics, like magic mushrooms (*Psilocybin*) and peyote cacti (*Mescaline*), were used by a good majority of their people.

In this culture, *among many others*, a spiritual aura surrounded magic mushrooms, and they were used to help their people *"communicate with the earth, the universe, the moon, especially the energy of the moon"*. A modern-day native (*to Oaxaca, Mexico*) continues, *"The mushroom shows you everything—about your errors, your problems, all the good you've done, all the bad you've done. It's something personal."*

But when the Western Christian Conquistadors entered the Mesoamerican realm, their cultural malware, defined by greed and materialism, not generosity and temperance, *"suppressed many aspects of traditional spiritual expression, including the use of mushrooms"* and peyote.[72]

As Dr. Ben Sessa, author of the *Psychedelic Renaissance*, states, what is "often called 'oceanic boundlessness', the psychedelic experience can trigger a sense of being part of a much wider entity than the traditional boundaries of personhood." Perhaps it's precisely this lack of control that incentivized Spanish conquistadors to construct an entirely negative perception of psychedelics.

Magic mushrooms and *"Peyote [were] unquestionably [some] of the most potent vision-inducing plants to be encountered by the conquerors, and the Conquistadors immediately began a program intended to suppress diabolical practices of the natives".*[73]

Their usage did not promote the conquistador's primary objective, conquering and controlling foreign territories. Magic mushrooms or peyote make people question the validity of their actions. Individuals with no interest in reconceptualizing the moral integrity of their doings would have no desire an engaging in an ASC defined by openness.

After Spanish conquistadors exerted their technological dominance over Mesoamerica, the collapse of civilizations like the Aztecs was inevitable. Under Spanish rule, the insurgence of magic mushroom usage was officially silenced, in which mushrooms began a three-century-long game of hide-and-seek. Fungal spores were only cultivated in the corners of society and much of their usage was done in secrecy. As such, continuing the psychedelic legacy within Mesoamerican culture became problematic.

The societal curtains of unpopularity came crashing down on Mesoamerica's spiritual industry and only underground ritual sites, cast away from the public eye, became places for mushroom consumption. While magic mushrooms were originally used at large-scale ceremonies and intended for people known as shamans, volunteers who were deemed worthy of becoming vessels to channel the mushroom's divine energy, with the presence of Spanish rulers, these ceremonies were whittled down to smaller and smaller groups until groups no larger than three or four would partake.

This became the new tradition until the early twentieth century, which unleashed the final tidal wave of the psychedelic's second wave—washing away the ancestral footprints that revealed humans' relationship with drugs like magic mushrooms (*amanita muscaria*).

It's important to remember (before we start making false assumptions like—*if psychedelics truly offered a cognitive edge to our species, one might think the Spanish conquistador's efforts should have resulted in failure*) that humans' relationship with these substances stretches far beyond the horizon of Mesoamerica. If this wasn't true, we could easily debunk the Stoned Ape Hypothesis proposed in Chapter 4 because a civilization emphasizing psychedelic consumption was just sacked by those that don't.

But it's not that simple. Psychedelics are used globally "*as staple commodities, by large segments of the population in a socially approved way*", sprouting from plants on all six or seven livable continents.

Observing Eurasian cultures, we see, "The mushroom **Amanita muscaria**, commonly known as fly agaric, has been at the center of religious rituals in Central Asia for at least 4000 years. Children know this beautiful white-spotted red mushroom from the illustrations of fairy tales and Christmas cards."

Or navigating south, "amanita muscaria had a religious significance in ancient India, and travelers recorded its use as late as the 18th century in Northeastern Siberia. It was an ingredient of Soma, a sacred beverage in the Rigveda in ancient India, and of Haoma, a sacred beverage mentioned in the Avesta, the ancient scriptures of Zoroastrianism".[74]

We've highlighted Mesoamerica culture as opposed to Ancient China or India, among the many others, because this was the first time in history that we see a complete suppression of drugs. While drug-restriction is a primary theme within early civilization as it allowed monopolies to form (*also a product of cultural malware*), drug-prohibition, at this level, was novel to the human species. When we travel to the final stop on the second wave of our psychedelic roller-coaster, this defining feature helps reveal why America's counter-culture movement is such a buzz-era. In this era, once again, control serves as the basis for America's Thoughtware, revitalizing our historical cultural malware with even more vigor than before.

THE WAR ON DRUGS

1986 featured an incredibly diverse set of historical events. We created a day to celebrate one of the many prominent spokespersons of the civil rights movement. We braced ourselves against the chaotic storms of radioactive debris forming in northern Europe. And in, inarguably, one of the most iconic national televised events in the world, Nancy Reagan advocated the "just say no" to drugs campaign. In the U.S., drugs became the object of satanic worship—a subclass of consumables that instilled terror among the general populace.

After Nancy Reagan's commentary—which placed taboos on drug consumption, long-haired hippies wearing tie-dyed shirts and sandals, 'hanging' out with a fresh bowl of hand-picked marijuana buds—*hippies* became just one of the many scapegoats throughout the 1960 and 1970s.

For example, television broadcasted "extensive coverage of gatherings organized by Timothy Leary and Ken Kesey", *two prominent spokespersons of the counter-culture rebellion*, "during which they encouraged and facilitated the open use of the hallucinogenic drug LSD." However, when these events were filmed, none of these substances were illegal. By design, all this captured footage was released after illegalizing their usage. In doing so, the public started to perceive the hippy lifestyle as if they were drug addicts—marijuana-crazed and psychedelic-infused radicals that were responsible for the sickness of American culture.

However, the media never told America that hippies were composed of many people no different from the rest, people who wanted to make the country better, more diversified and resilient to violence, as they protested, *"Make Love, Not War"* or *"U.S. Troops Get Out of Vietnam"*.[75]

It's interesting that this group was led by professors and intellectuals like Timothy Leary, a psychologist at Harvard University, Alfred Hubbard (*also known as the original Captain Trip*), who introduce more than 6,000 people to LSD, and Aldous Huxley, famous through his novel *Brave New World*.

These individuals wouldn't be categorized as anarchists without some type of external intervention. They treated psychedelics very seriously, and their "ennobling idea… forgotten or lost in the visual scene, diverted by chemistry, was their plan for community," as stated by Mark Harris, a journalist for *The Atlantic Times*, in 1967.[76]

But as their opinions quickly became glamorized and metamorphosized by both the American media and those who misinterpreted their root philosophy, the malevolent genius behind America's artificially generated stereotype of the hippies started to take form.

Over the next few decades, media always portrayed hippies exhaling a potent THC (the active ingredient in *weed)* vapor cloud, 'dropping' LSD, and ranting about the conspiratorial nature of society. Loading up their next bowl of hand-picked marijuana buds, they might become more aggressive as their drug-addiction starts kicking in—craving that next hit and urging others to "rebel against the system.... man" or "do away with those capitalist pigs."

They became the objects of ridicule, desperate individuals who have already made a deal with the devil, stating, "I'll give you my life if you give me a shot of heroin or a bump of the finest crack cocaine."

However, in the same year that Nancy Reagan initiated the **War on Drugs** with the launch of the "Just Say No" campaign, while mass media started synthesizing and televising anarchist-like stereotypes about hippies, President Ronald Reagan signed off on a deal to promote the export of prescription drugs.

Something doesn't add up here. Among all the rebellious groups in American history, the hippie culture led the most peaceful rebellion. In addition, why should the general population "just say no" to drugs when the president and his administration say yes?

Why should we blindly accept the criticism drugs when, behind the scenes, the people sitting on the top of our societal power hierarchy are dealing drugs in bulk?

In other words, what if the "War on Drugs" was just a route to ensure the prosperity of a political agenda?

Behind the scenes, American politicians were struggling to prevent the polarization of culture. At the top of the power hierarchy, individuals became control-crazed not because of hippies but because of (1) the cultural pressures induced by radical minorities that made up the Civil Rights Movement and (2) the Vietnam War, which raged on as the chaotic jungles of Vietnam, filled with strong-armed nationalistic Viet Cong soldiers, claimed the lives of millions.

Looking for a way to mediate riots both inside and outside borders, policy leaders had no time to deal with fact; rather, they had to figure out how to create fiction, a scapegoat to blame for the disorderly cultural climate. In doing so, they could then focus their efforts on war-time pursuits.

To solve these problems, the War on Drugs became a novel solution, and from 1968 to 1978, with the illegalization of LSD in 1968, labeling it as a schedule I under the Controlled Substances Act, followed by the Convention on Psychotropics Substances (CPS) United Nations treaty in 1971, and ending with the Psychotropic Substances Act of 1978, all publicly known psychedelics became criminalized and strictly mandated.

In an interview with Brad Burge, the current communication director for MAPS, he explains the rationale behind this law:

"Why they wanted to criminalize it so badly was specifically because they realized that there were these groups of people in the country that were resistant to the administration, resistant to Vietnam, resistant to the Nixon White House policies, and they realized that it couldn't criminalize people, but they could criminalize the drugs that they were using."

And keep in mind, not just psychedelics were outlawed. To target a much larger set of individuals, these acts also outlawed all amphetamine-type stimulants, barbiturates, and benzodiazepines—chemicals that share relatively little chemical features with one another and have drastically different effects on human biology.

Throughout the long and arduous process that came with drug illegalization, control was the only desire that fueled American policy and law enforcement. In effect, just like when Spanish conquistadors suppressed psychedelics, America had revived conquistador's cultural malware and reprogrammed it to account for human behavior in the modern era—creating the newest version, **Cultural Malware V2.0.**

CULTURAL MALWARE V2.0

With this cultural malware now installed in the American government, we can finally understand why hippies became perfect targets to blame for America's cultural sickness.

Hippies engaged in activities openly and were well known by the public. Tipped off by the government, the media began developing stereotypes to transition the public's attention toward hippies.

The reason?

Due to the tender cultural climate surrounding racial inequality, the American government didn't want people to see who their true targets were—ethnic minorities.

As Burge states, *"Cannabis and psychedelics were associated with political radicals and ethnic minorities, and both of these groups of people were seen by the white house as enemies of the state, and yes–ethnic minorities were enemies of the state."*

In other words, much of the taboos surrounding drugs were not derived due to their toxicity but because the taboos themselves became effective political tools to control a demographic of people. To this day, the effectiveness of the War on Drugs continues to be one of the sole reasons the majority of people in jail are of a single (1) political party and (2) racial background.[77]

For example, if we break down a population of one hundred people who smoke marijuana, we find that nearly eighty-seven of them will be Democrats, helping us understand why people in jail consist of a single political party.[78]

Furthermore, the Controlled Substances Act continues to behave like an ethnicity-seeking missile because of this same population. A 2012 study found that fifty-five out of one hundred marijuana smokers are black, which is why we see people in jail consisting of a single racial background.[79]

In other words, by lumping a whole host of drugs into schedule I, *a class of drugs reserved for substances with no accepted medical use and a high potential for abuse*, local law enforcement can throw people caught for possession behind bars or give them a felony charge. In both situations, an overwhelming majority will lose their right to vote.* This is the key idea behind the government's cultural malware-guided plan.

Richard Nixon, the president during this era, mandated a Republican legislation, and now it's no mystery why outlawing marijuana, among a whole host of other drugs, proved highly effective in decreasing political resistance from *enemies of the state—ethnic minorities.*

*Note: In America, Individuals are ineligible to vote with a
Felony in 35/50 states or as an Inmate in 48/50 states.

But telling the public about this plan would only add fuel to cultural fires, so the Nixon administration sold their *'Just say No'* slogan with claims that deliberately target a key component in human rationale—**safety.**

Here's one made by the DEA about LSD in 1999:

"Although initial observations on the benefits of LSD were highly optimistic, empirical data developed subsequently proved less promising ... Its use in scientific research has been extensive and its use has been widespread.

Although the study of LSD and other hallucinogens increased the awareness of how chemicals could affect the mind, its use in psychotherapy largely has been debunked. It produces no aphrodisiac effects, does not increase creativity, has no lasting positive effect in treating alcoholics or criminals, does not produce a 'model psychosis,' and does not generate immediate personality change".[80]

But claims like these only reached older audiences, so to make sure this cultural malware also transpired into the next version of America's generational software, the DARE program was launched. Burge recalls, "I remember when I was in school, and I went through the DARE program, the whole "just say no" program.

We had a police officer come and reclaim the ban—drugs taken from the drug dealers they busted, and they taught all the kids that if somebody offers you drugs, just say no.

No matter what.

The impression they left us with was always "smart people have done research, and we have found that these drugs are bad and that these drugs are good."

In fact, most people don't know we found out many years later that there never was any research".

When psychedelic experts—including the founder of MAPS, Rick Doblin—called BS on these claims, it was already too late. Cultural malware v2.0 had already been installed into America's cultural software.

More specifically, Burge continues, *"The controlled Substances Act, which placed LSD, MDMA, psilocybin and a whole host of other drugs into this category—the most restrictive possible category and the most stigmatizing category had **nothing to do with research**. There's already been a significant amount of research, and a lot of that research was presented at some of the original hearing.*

For example, the original hearing in 1985, Rick Doblin and a lot of experts testified with the DEA that MDMA should not be moved to schedule one. It has a medical and therapeutic use and there had been substantial research and MDMA studies to support that, but then the DEA completely ignored all of that scientific testimony and moved it to Schedule one anyway–just because of these irrational fears, you know—oh my God, the children!"

And here's the kicker of it all. In 2016, former Nixon domestic policy chief, John Ehrlichman admits:

"We knew we couldn't make it illegal to be either against the war or black, but by getting the public to **associate the hippies with marijuana and blacks with heroin and then criminalizing both heavily, we could disrupt those communities.** We could arrest their leaders, raid their homes, break up their meetings, and vilify them night after night on the evening news. **Did we know we were lying about the drugs? Of course, we did."**

But even with this information, it was already too late.

Psychedelics criminalization in the second wave had already culturally mutated the public's perception of these substances. Its association with the chaos and civil disobedience within America constructed firm roots, and with it, rigid taboos.

It's important to note that I'm not arguing that all claims about LSD and other psychedelics are false, but before we place strict taboos on these groups of chemicals, we should at least be able to back them up.

Without these rigid taboos in place, we can perhaps absorb statements made by Terrence Mckenna with a heightened level of clarity, like:

"Psychedelics are illegal not because a loving government is concerned that you may jump out of a third-story window.

Psychedelics are illegal because they **dissolve opinion structures** and **culturally laid down models of behavior** and information processing. **They open you up to the possibility that everything you know is wrong.**"

And the reason Mark Haden, a University of British Columbia professor, states, "We've exaggerated the harms of drugs, we've never acknowledged the benefits of drugs, and we've never talked about the dominant model for controlling drugs in our society, which is drug prohibition, which has failed us all so badly".[81]

While the second wave might be the bumpiest journey on our psychedelic roller coaster, as we navigate to the next wave, we'll find that people have started to approach these substances more delicately and responsibly in the third wave.

CHAPTER 6

THE THIRD WAVE

——

Now in 2019, we have once again begun to look to psychedelics for answers. While public awareness about psychedelics died down in the last fifty to sixty, years, those that clung to the second wave operated underground, waiting for the right moment to leap us into a third wave.

That mousetrap has been sprung, and we have officially entered the beginnings of the third wave, only this time, with a bit more wisdom. As more evidential-based arguments see the light of day, many others have begun to step out from the shadows.

After realizing the mistakes made in the second wave, the modern psychedelic community has started to make tremendous progress in building an objective and well-respected opinion around psychedelic drugs. Over the last sixty years, technology has progressed exponentially, and with them, our abilities to conceptualize how these chemicals affect the mind.

Books like *"How to Change Your Mind"* by Michael Pollan and scientific research by MAPS are being published every year, and with them, the newest version of humanity's generational software is finding its way into the growing psychedelic community. Online forums like Erowid and Reddit have sprouted their own niche communities in which we see open discussions about the utility of psychedelics being taken more seriously.

Online journals and magazines are starting to reopen the psychedelic conversation. And as laws about marijuana use grow weaker throughout the U.S., so too does the political opposition against decriminalizing psychedelics, with the influx of psychedelic research pointing out these substances' untapped potential. just this past year, Denver, Colorado, has already taken a leading charge in becoming the first U.S. city to decriminalize psilocybin mushrooms.

Johns Hopkins University just opened the first official psychedelic research center in 2019, with nearly $17 million in research grants from venture capitalists who also look toward psychedelics' future optimistically.[82]

Now that sixty years have passed, the third wave has hit America, only this time with a much more rationally minded approach to understanding these chemically induced states.

A RATIONAL APPROACH

While the first half of this book was most closely associated with the observable, long-term inter- and intra-personal effects that psychedelics have had on humans, the next portion will be dedicated to exploring what the psychedelic experience really is—what's happening neurologically?

Why do people like Stanislav Grof, one of the founders of transpersonal psychology, or Rick Doblin think LSD, *"if properly used could become something like the microscope or telescope of psychiatry"*?[83]

Why is it important to stress the *proper* and *responsible* use of psychedelics and what untold dangers lie in the wake if we don't listen to these words of wisdom?

In other words, how can humans *effectively* use psychedelics to achieve a Mind Leap?

Because these questions are incredibly difficult to answer, we will navigate through the psychedelic experience objectively, leaving behind the subjective baggage filled with stories like "meeting alien beings" and epiphanies like "I now know the **true** meaning of the universe".

While these stories do have value for the individual, rarely do they help us construct a way to understand the experience from the outside—a collective interpretation. Instead, we will opt for a more rational approach by realizing that each psychedelic stimulates the human mind in different ways, generating an ASC with unique features and diverse utility.

In addition, by sifting through neurological studies of the brain with modern biotechnologies like fMRIs (*functional Magnetic Resonance Imaging*) and EEGs (Electroencephalography), we can pinpoint regions of the brain and speculate about what interactions give rise to different operational modes of our Thoughtware.

In this sense, we will realize that human Thoughtware can operate at many frequencies both with and without ingesting psychedelics—which, in turn, serves as a baseline for which we can unveil unique **Frames of Mind** that our current Thoughtware resides in.

FRAMES OF MIND

The first thing to emphasize is that a frame of mind is broader in scope than an ASC. An ASC is just one potential version of human Thoughtware, while each frame of mind can encompass multiple versions.

For example, as mentioned throughout this book, we know humans can obtain many ASCs. While some might help us understand our current mood *(through mediation or fasting)* by turning on introspective personality traits, others help us solve problems outside of our skin that require cooperation *(through dancing or religion)* by turning on extravertive personality traits.

In other words, depending on what inter- or intra-personal problem we're trying to solve, human Thoughtware exhibits different communicatory properties. When communicating with others, an extrovertive process, we speak an entirely different language than we do with ourselves, an introvertive process. And we can observe this effect by further breaking down human Thoughtware into two separate components, the upper level, *generational and cultural software*, and the lower level, *genetic and environmental software*. For now, it might be easiest to represent the upper level as our *conscious* software and the lower level as our *unconscious* software.

UPPER-LEVEL OF THOUGHTWARE

In the context of communicating with others, when we visited color language, we realized that some cultures use a frame of mind dedicated to **association**, like using the sky to categorize the color blue. On the other hand, cultures like the Hanunoo people prefer a **deconstructive** frame of mind, breaking down reflection and absorption properties of light into a metric of light versus darkness and wetness versus dryness.

Take, for instance, the frame of mind required to read this book. The letters you're reading are merely shapes, yet if we speak the language of literacy, we intuitively understand that with enough letters, these shapes become words, and words—sentences and so on. But letters, words, and sentences, just like color, are figments of your imagination, cultural place-holders for the world, that attempt to communicate the abstract phenomenon that encircles us.

To read at a comprehensive level and speak the language of literacy, once again, the mind operates in a different frame. This time, we opt for a **constructive** frame of mind as we compile the symbols of writing into high-level forms of communication.

Furthermore, in Chapter 5, we loosely discussed ancient culture's use of religion and government, languages of order, that use a frame of mind concerned with **morality** and **ethicality** to enforce law and righteousness. By shifting into this frame of mind, our capabilities to describe things that exist outside of sensory perception are heightened. Things like theocracy, communistic dictatorships, and liberal democracies, products of our imagination, bear fruits from the labors of this language.

However, the language of color, literacy, and order are not hardwired into the human-animal. They are embedded within a collective's generational software, the highest level of humans' Thoughtware. To achieve fluency in these languages, individuals must install a region's cultural software and use it to speak the most up-to-date version of the language. For example, in America, English is the most commonly spoken language.

Therefore, it is well ingrained into America's cultural software, but to speak this language at a modern level, which includes all the newest terms, like *software* and *hardware,* and slang, like *Lit (something cool)* or *Fam (circle of close friends),* one must learn the generational software.

For these same reasons, we chose to conceptualize the brain and mind as hardware and Thoughtware. Neuroscience and psychology deal with an extremely abstract phenomenon, many of which we still can't communicate accurately. Therefore, it's quite clear why the language of neuroscience and psychology is far different from a few centuries ago.

For example, in the 1700s, steam engines dominated the technology industry. In this era, they were the most complex entities humans had conceptualized. So people like G.W. Leibniz would use the generational software of this time period and say, *"If we were magically shrunk and put into someone's brain while she was thinking, we would see all the pumps, pistons, gears and levers working away, and we would be able to describe their workings completely, in mechanical terms, thereby completely describing the thought processes of the brain.*

But that description would nowhere contain any mention of thought! It would contain nothing but descriptions of pumps, pistons, levers!"

However, since *thought was still not communicated*, as mechanical contraptions were replaced with digital technologies in the 1950s, we then updated our generational software to account for this missing communication link. Now, it's rather common to describe the brain and mind using computer-science jargon. By observing similarities between digital technologies and the function of the brain and mind, jargon like hardware and Thoughtware become helpful terms to communicate meaning behind these structures.

And we see this effect rippling across all different languages. Inside an exponential society, science, technology, and business are evolving every-day and when our attention diverts from one of these fields for just a few moments, our ability to speak their modern language escapes us.

In other words, instead of revising the basic form of communication to conceptualize the new, complex information we've obtained, we're still using the ancient language of speech. In effect, we're seeing the reprogramming of a top-heavy Thoughtware hierarchy. And we know from Chapter 1 that the Egyptian pyramids are still around today because they were built from the bottom up (right-side up pyramid) not the top down (inverted pyramid).

For this reason, most students are not graduating in four years. Instead, we see that 60 percent of students will take six years to graduate and learn modern languages.[84] With so much content and information unleashed into the public atmosphere, what took people four years to learn, say ten years ago, is now taking six years. In another ten years, this might increase to eight years, and so on.

Alas! This is the basic dilemma that comes with over-specialization, in which individuals will become obsessed with updating just one language. But in the process, they've trapped themselves from speaking the other less technical and more collaborative languages, and it's only a matter of time before their Thoughtware topples over. An inverted triangle lacks stability.

That's the major problem!

Our *conscious* upper levels of Thoughtware are not built for the dynamic nature of our society. For example, the human brain can perform nearly 38 thousand trillion computations per second (38 petraflops–10x10^15). To give you an idea of how incredible this is, only five supercomputers in the world can top our brain's speed (the fastest being *Summit,* which has an estimated delivery of 200 petraflops).[85]

However, of humans' vast computational power, 99.99 percent of computations are done in the lower levels of our Thoughtware.[86] For this reason, if we want to shift our frames of mind and learn new languages more effectively, we must turn our attention toward the lower-levels of Thoughtware. That's where the true power of humans' cognitive adaptability lies. And it's not as though humans have never realized this. Early sapiens have been aware of this idea, even without their knowing, of the computational breakdown between the upper and lower levels.

LOWER-LEVELS OF THOUGHTWARE

How have humanity's lower levels of Thoughtware evolved?

The main contrasting element between ancient and modern Thoughtware stems from the use of lower levels of Thoughtware. The genius behind ancient society's Thoughtware is that they realized how to speak these fundamental languages effectively. They learned the languages of the body that exist within our environmental and genetic software. As a result, they deliberately sought frames of mind that transcended verbal communication and connected communities on a deeper level, as Michael Winkelman eludes.

"Rhythmic **dancing, marching, clapping,** and **chanting** were **central aspects of ancient socialization**… that integrated individuals' sensory experience "in a way that intrinsically links individuals into a **cooperative community**. The rhythmic motions and emotional vocalizations (music) **enhanced cooperation as nonverbal communication systems** for bonding groups beyond the family".[87]

In other words, they used languages of dancing, marching, clapping, and chanting to communicate. Interestingly psychedelics were often consumed when engaged in these ritualistic practices.

We might be quick to invoke the question, what role did psychedelics play in this process?

But, we're not there yet. It's not as though psychedelics were mandatory consumables in these types of communication environments. They just amplified the connective qualities of these languages.

While we might be quick to assume that these languages are rather primitive, because nowadays, we have access to instantaneous communication devices—high-speed cellular towers that unleash optimized bits of data at a moment's notice—I might argue that digital messages are far more primitive forms of language. They are shallow and easily misinterpreted because, even though we can shoot messages across the globe, the amount of information they contain is relatively little.

It's nearly impossible to know the emotional state of the person who sent the message and its context— hence the abuse of emojis in the digital era to that aim to mediate this problem. But it seems to me that they only add more layers of abstraction. Given the vast expanse of emotional states a human can experience, it seems obvious to say there is no digital spreadsheet of symbols that can encompasses human expression better than face-face interaction. ;)

Without this data, our ability to decipher the emotional encryption of communication becomes far less effective.

For example, a study done back in the 1970s by Albert Mehrabian suggests "that we overwhelmingly deduce our feelings, attitudes, and beliefs about what someone says not by the actual words spoken, but by the speaker's body language and tone of voice".[88] After observing how much information people could send through three different mediums—spoken words, voice and tone, and body language—they broke down the importance of each medium. They found that only 7 percent of meaning was interpreted by spoken words, 38 percent by tone, and 55 percent by body language.

That's why if someone says, "I don't have a problem with you"— "while avoiding eye-contact, looking anxious, and maintaining closed body language", the listener will disregard the spoken words and interpret the message conveyed by the body. And we do this *unconsciously* because a deeper language is being spoken, a language that our conscious minds can't really put into words. And yet so much meaning is lost without these mediums of communication.

This concept prevailed within early hominid societies, and it's why dancing and chanting were highly effective to build community and collaborative networks. They incentivized body language, pitch, and tone to express their interpretation of reality. They used the hidden language embedded within the human-animal's lower levels that can transmit far more information about the world than the upper levels. It is the unconscious language of instinct, which can become an extremely effective language to help us shift our frame of mind and understand others better, but on the other hand, without realizing its power, it can also restrict us from achieving new ones.

For example, when we perceive the weather as hot or cold or sense over-arching threats of danger, the language of instinct boots up our genetic software's 'fight or flight' programs, which, in turn, suppresses our ability to shift into a different frame of mind. Normally, when a 20-caliber pistol's barrel is pressed against a human's head, rationality quickly escapes.

On the contrary, our frame of mind is suddenly outside of our control as our instincts boot up our survivability program, consuming each layer of Thoughtware in the process. Settings that ensure trust and safety are crucial components of developing complex languages and cultural adaptability. Without them, a hidden language starts taking over, a language of instinct.

For example, in education, trust and safety are the essential pillars. Without these components students easily become distracted by the language of instinct, triggering worry and anxiety. Therefore, schools are mandated to do routine natural disaster, school shooting, or evacuation drills. It quells the instinctual urges of both the students, perhaps unconsciously, and the parents, so that both can maintain a frame of mind necessary for daily tasks.

And that's not to say the language of instinct is purely detrimental to our frame of mind. Rather, it's highly valuable so long as you're aware of what triggers it. Our genetic software comes with five built-in languages—the language of touch, smell, taste, sound, and sight—that help us open dialogues with the world we live in.

For example, by learning the vibrational language of sound, we can identify the presence of moving objects, or more historically, incoming predators. Learning the nutritional language of taste, we can break down foreign substrates into sweetness, saltiness, sourness, bitterness, and umami to decipher potential sources of toxin or poison, and the list goes on for each sense. I'll leave you to decipher what types of language stem from our other sensory faculties.

In the context of dancing (among other historical connective language), we realize specific traits of others by observing their dance technique. In this sense, dancing becomes a tool to erect a medium of transparency between two individuals, in which a mutual agreement about their internal states, motivations, and desires are communicated through diverse body movements. It's a conversation spoken in the language of instinct, and that's why it's nearly impossible to communicate the same amount of information that a dance move does in comparison to just a few text messages. In other words, a wealth of insights can be obtained by our sensory perceptions.

In effect, it is more accurate to say that instinct is a language that helps us plug into the environmental software of our world.

It connects all the loose stimuli we obtain from the environment—internalizes them in the lower levels of our

Thoughtware, and overtime, as this communication starts to work its way up the hierarchy, suddenly, a thought is auto populated in the upper-levels, a "gut feeling". We get this feeling not because we're consciously interpreting something; rather, our bodies have internalized and interpreted it for us without our knowing.

Not only does it help us understand the world we inhabit but also the biological vehicles that we drive around in each day.

Intra-personally, the language of instinct is more closely associated with the voice of reason in our minds. It is concerned with self-betterment and self-discipline, one that describes the core elements that define our purpose in life.

Most of the time we base nearly all our decisions and preferences on this language of instinct. It tells us the types of people we prefer, foods that are good for us, and distinct goals we want to achieve.

However, as languages that priorities the use of the body increasingly become defined as relics from primitive civilizations with the advance of technologies that enable international communication, it becomes all too easy to forget the language of instinct without using it on a daily basis.

So, what happens when we forget the language of instinct?

What's important to keep reinforcing is that that current version of human Thoughtware is not too dissimilar from the ancestral version. It's not as though forgetting the language of instinct is a problem unique to the 21st century. Rather communication is a timeless human dilemma. The only difference in today's version of Thoughtware is that humans have become more skeptical of engaging in activities that drastically alter their mental acuity. One factor might be due to increase in a society's population. The greater the population, the greater the variety. The greater the variety, the more rules and regulations needed to maintain a controlled social climate.

However, from an ancestral perspective, populations sizes were much smaller, in which rules and regulations were organized a communal basis and not so grossly generalized. In this respect, these smaller communities were less timid to cognitive alteration. They knew if they wanted to connect on a deeper level and transition their frame of thinking into one more apt for spiritual enlightenment or communal growth, they must seek routes to regain or explore the language of instinct.

Hence why psychedelic ingestion (among many other various methods to achieve altered states of consciousness) were essentials in early societies and why psychotropics became the bread and butter served at the ancestral dinner table.[89]

Unable to connect at the local dancing or chanting ceremonies?

3.5g of psilocybin mushrooms might remedy the dilemma.

But what's the hard truth about these chemicals?

What's happening neurologically when psychedelics are consumed and how does this bring us to a greater understanding about psychedelics place both in ancestral and modern societies?

Now, aided by modern neuroscience technologies, we can loosely explain why psychedelics allowed them to tap into this network of insight and realize the temporality of the information contained within the upper levels of Thoughtware. It's time we venture into our mental hardware to explain this phenomenon in depth.

MENTAL HARDWARE

The brain is a dynamic system with ever-changing electrical activity. It is equipped with a huge array of electric hubs, neurons, and cellular switches that can turn these neurons on or off at a moment's notice—receptors. In controlling these reactions efficiently, the brain has become humanity's most valuable tool for rapid information collection and organization. However, because your brain processes information differently than my own, if we wanted to engage in a conversation, we wouldn't get very far by describing our present neural activity.

For simplicity, say both of us are just neural software programs, composed of just three neurons, A, B, and C. As software programs, we exist in a virtual reality, in other words, we don't have bodies to communicate with.

With only three neurons, we can only perform a few communication programs, in which each time a program initiates, one of my neurons sends a signal to a different one.

For example, one of my programs communicates the idea *"let's be friends"* by shooting a signal from my neuron A to neuron B.

But your neural software is wired differently than mine. Instead, your A to B connection means *let's be enemies*. So after shooting a signal from my neuron A to B and sending this information to you, we both walk away feeling confused, as little information was traded without any form of body language to interpret what my A to B signal means. So while one of us thinks we're friends, you think we're enemies.

We now have a word to represent this frequent interaction, and I'm sure you're familiar with it— **miscommunication**. In the case of three neurons, it might be easy to understand that it was a simple miscommunication, but when we add nearly one hundred billion neurons to the mix, the complexity of our miscommunication takes on a whole new level.

We observed that we become highly apt to misinterpret digital messages. It's like we're only using three neuronal routes to communicate, when our human body can interpret a much larger chunk of information. In other words, we're restricting our communication abilities, wasting our precious attention on communicating with shallow information bits.

But in the same sense, we're not just receiving one or two text messages at a time. On the contrary, we're receiving hundreds of online notifications every single day, and so the need to simplify becomes rather imperative.

However, I think that's flawed logic because often much redundancy in the information floods our upper levels. Not to mention the sheer amount of ingroup and conformationally biased information that uses these simplified mediums of language to manipulate people.

For example, back in 2016, a Russian agency controlled by the Kremlin hired many individuals to start unique Facebook pages. In total, publicly known at least, this agency had created nearly 500 Facebook pages to target unique sets of individuals and plant seeds of misinformation. They realized that to manipulate Facebook users in Europe and Central Asia, they could target specific niche communities by posting "religious" or "governmentally" based memes. They would post a picture of "Jesus" or whatever religion dogma their niche community believed in, with a caption saying, *"Trust in Jesus".*

In turn, they would build up their Facebook community pages, and after achieving X many page subscribers, they started including subliminal messages in each of their posts. By associating their words with religious dogma, they could then influence small groups of individuals to vote in a specific way, since it's what "Jesus" would want—hence why ingroup biases are so powerful.

As the *New York Times* states, *"Facebook said one of the campaigns had targeted people in 13 countries in Eastern Europe and Central Asia. Facebook deleted 289 pages and 75 accounts linked to that effort, which also spent about $135,000 on Facebook advertising from 2013 to 2019.*

The company said the misleading content aimed to influence people in Armenia, Azerbaijan, Estonia, Georgia, Kazakhstan, Kyrgyzstan, Latvia, Lithuania, Moldova, Romania, Russia, Tajikistan, and Uzbekistan".[90]

This might sound familiar to what happened in the 1960s.

Once again, we see people placing too much faith in the upper levels of their Thoughtware.

And on a neurological level, we can see why this happens.

* * *

Inside the neural mixture of our brain, we have a power called **neural plasticity**, which helps us exchange the communicatory information we receive from the environment and transform the meaning of it into something more culturally viable.

Let's look back at our three-neuron software example and see why this ability has led us so far as a species. Say, for example, all your friends are in alignment with your neural wiring and you all think that an A to C connection means let's be enemies. Instead of having to over complicate each of our interactions by telling you my A to C is really your A to B connection, the human brain has the capability to rewire specific neural connections.

With enough reinforcement and over a prolonged period, my A to C connection will unconsciously rewire itself to align with the group's internal definition. So when you introduce me to your friends, we can more easily come to mutual agreements about our relations with one another.

Now, of course, when we're looking at a *non-simplified* brain, it's not that simple; however, the idea remains the same.

Neural plasticity is just a way of describing our brain's ability to change continuously throughout the course of our lives. In the above example, we observed a **functional** change in my neuron A to C connection. However, neural plasticity also allows us to make **structural** changes in our brains. It's the same idea as going to the gym. The more neuron A sends a signal to C, the faster and more permanent the signal strength becomes. On an evolutionary level, it seems rather apparent why this would aid in our survival.

It helps build larger communities as more individuals become capable of opening dialogues with others. However, as more individuals start to follow along, our human brain starts to trust the tribe instead of its original version of interpretation, and we approach a very dangerous idea.

What if the prevailing interpretation in these niche communities is wrong?

However, people inside this community will assume that it can't possibly be wrong because so many people are in agreement—hence the formation of a group bias. But in Russia, they took advantage of this idea. They realized that they could create hundreds of fake accounts and comment on each post, continually reinforcing that the content being posted was accurate and in bounds with the community goals. In this sense, manipulation was once again spawned by installing cultural malware in the human brain, just like in the 1960s about the world's perceptions of drugs.

According to Johan E. Korteling, *"If human thinking does not show some internalized form of extensional, classical logic where it should conform to such a normative standard, human rationality is brought into question. If alternative normative systems are not available or arbitrary there is little ground for deriving unifying laws of cognition from a set of basic axioms".*[91]

In other words, if we become like stray ducks and start seeking any 'ol mother duck to take us under their wing, the formation of group biases starts to form. Instead of tapping into their unconscious network, thinking back and attempting to search for their true mother duck (using *internalized, classic logic)*, they will absorb whatever generational software comes their way because it's easy and they don't have to think (since *alternative systems are not available)*. They just learn the new language and move on with their life.

And like we said, after spending years being a part of this group, the prevailing ideas within the groups start to become hardwired through neural plasticity in the human brain.

But like I've reinforced continually through this book, not knowing how to use a tool, like neural plasticity, is a surefire way for abuse to follow. Neural plasticity is a tool that can be used in good ways as well.

For example, neural plasticity has molded the unique abilities of the *sea-nomad* children who live along the west coast of Thailand in a tribe known as the *Moken* people. From a young age, these children would routinely make dives into the ocean to collect clams, shells, and sea cucumbers (*reinforcement*). While underwater, their eyes would be wide open, scanning the natural environment of the coastal floor. At first glance, you might think that constantly stimulating these children's eyes with the high salinity waters of the ocean would deteriorate their ability to see.

However, a study done by Anna Gislen in 1999 revealed that, in comparison to a population of European children, "Moken children were able to see twice as well." In reinforcing this routine on a consistent basis, these children became more apt to see underwater. Neurologically, these children had initiated a call to neural plasticity, effectively rewiring the neurons that allowed them to see.[92]

So when these children were granted better underwater sight, it was not necessarily a change in the eye itself, but a reactionary change granted through neural plasticity.

Every day, they were putting their environmental software to work by soaking their eyes in high salinity waters and unconsciously speaking the language of instinct, telling their body that better eyesight was a necessity for their survival. However, even after reading this information, I doubt most people will start preparing a bath of saltwater every day to soak their eyeballs.

While changing your environment, as in the case of the Moken children, or joining a group, in the case of Russia's Facebook scam, can initiate neural plasticity, we can mold our present frame of minds in many others ways if we figure out how to tap into the high-processing power of the unconscious components of our mental hardware.

Luckily, there's a reason so many people are becoming interested in the science of the third wave of the psychedelic revolution. Psychedelics are a tool to help us open the language of instinct, call upon neural plasticity, and shift our frame mind more effectively to achieve a Mind Leap in our desired fields.

If in disbelief or cautious about these types of claims, perfect. Without knowledge of how drugs affect the neurological structures of the human, we should always be extremely meticulous, especially when it comes to their consumption. So let's break this down with the help of a well-known model, called *The Triune Brain,* which may unveil the neurological value of psychedelics and give us one route to tie up all the loose ends and questions we've proposed throughout this Chapter and book.

THE TRIUNE BRAIN

In the 1960s, American neuroscientist Paul MacLean attempted to divide humans' mental hardware into three distinct regions (1) the reptilian or **primal brain** (Basal Ganglia), (2) the paleo-mammalian or **emotional brain** (limbic system), and (3) the neo-mammalian or **rational brain**.

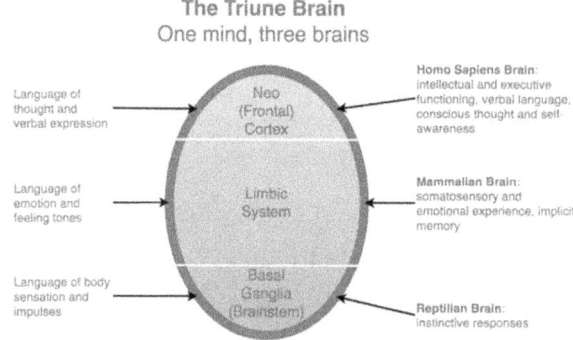

MacLean's Triune Brain model separates three regions of the brain by their respective functions.[93]

What's interesting about this model is that it proposes that the human brain is a hybrid piece of mental hardware, mimicking the structure of the reptilian brain (*primal brain*) to control our instinctual tendencies, integrating the old paleo-mammalian brains (*emotional brain)* to control our sensory and emotional experience, and adding on the new-est homo-sapien component (*rational brain*) to control our higher-level thinking.

In conjunction with our Thoughtware model, we can per-haps identify a few commonalities, in which our upper-level Thoughtware arises from the rational brain, the *conscious* programs, while our lower-level Thoughtware arises from both the primal and emotional brain.

From this information, we find that the unconsciously man-dated structures, primal and emotional brain, are those constantly sifting through infinite arrays of information inscribed into the world. In these regions, 99.99 percent of the human brain's computational power lies.

They are synched up to all our sensory devices and over-see the interpretation of nearly all information that courses through our central nervous system, an extremely long struc-ture stretching nearly 60,000 miles—more than twice the distance around the Earth! However, because so much infor-mation is constantly computed within these two complexes, the brain has evolved to restrict the flow of information from the older structures to the newest one.

In doing so, only the most relevant chunks of information will be sent to the higher-level brain structure—things like disgust, fear, happiness, sadness, and aggression—the fundamental emotional states, when an outside stimulus triggers them.

It does this through a chemically mandated process, biochemical changes in neurotransmitters, nutrients, and the list goes on and on. By doing so, humans' mental hardware can develop a real-time reactionary system depending on specific environmental influences—hence why our environmental software is so incredibly complex.

But the interesting thing is our brain has evolved in a world flooded with chemicals that can change the restrictive nature of the boundary lying between the older and newest structures. For this reason, diet, exercise, and drugs (among many other activities) impact how information courses through the human brain.

For example, a study conducted by the Imperial College London furthered this idea by scanning a variety of different people with (75 *micrograms*) and without LSD.

They used the popular neuro-imaging device, an MRI, to describe how different regions of neural activity react while in LSD-induced states of consciousness. They found that the brain "lights up" like a pine tree in December as an individual's neural map suddenly becomes interconnected.

Researchers observed neurons communicating with one another "as if the drug reversed restrictive thinking".[94]

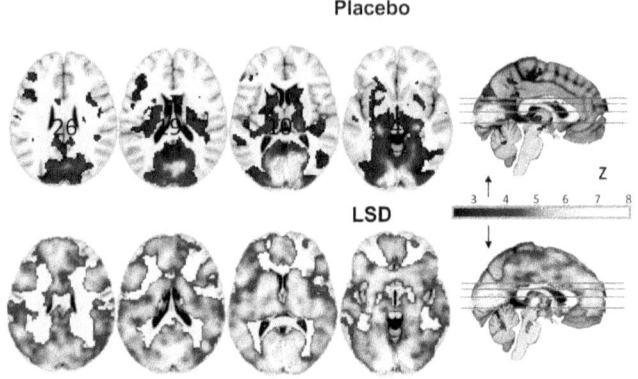

A second image shows different sections of the brain, either on placebo or under the influence of LSD (lot's of white/light grey). In this image, increasing whiteness indicates an increase in brain activity. Photograph: Imperial/Beckley Foundation

From these images of the brain, we can distinguish a very clear discrepancy between the two individuals. We see that in the placebo individual's brain, normal activity exists in the primal brain region (*the small portion of the brain lit up*), which makes sense because this system is constantly interpreting the environment using its environmental software. On the other hand, we also see that the lack of activity elsewhere suggests that the restrictive biochemical barrier is in place. This means that information from the unconscious brain is not flooding the conscious one, the frontal cortex (the upper portion of the brain).

However, in the LSD individual's brain, we see something drastically different, or as Robin Carhart-Harris, who led the study, states, "In many ways, the brain in the LSD state resembles the state our brains were in when we were infants: free and unconstrained." In other words, we're seeing that LSD is unlocking the biochemical barrier and not only stimulating the older structures but also allowing information obtained from them to flow into the newest one.

After looking at this image, it makes sense why LSD-ingestion makes individuals have a heightened sensory and emotional experience because the lower structures of the brain become stimulated. And in the conscious structure, it makes sense why people often characterize their experience as *providing understanding, enlightenment, a sense of unity and oneness with universe, feeling of connection with others, and personal integration.*

All the information normally simplified into a "gut-feeling" becomes accessible as much of the unconsciously interpreted information floods the frontal cortex of the individual, and suddenly they can process information about the world at a much higher level.

And it doesn't stop there; while many structures of the brain are stimulated by these psychedelics, one region of the brain is inhibited, the default mode network (DMN). And we know this network rather well. In general, this is the component of the brain that generates a version of the human known as the ego, a self-interpreting region that more loosely attempts to tell humans who and what they are (*self-consciousness*).[95]

And when this network is inhibited, **the ego dissolves**, which also makes sense why people report a feeling of "rebirth" after a psychedelic experience. Quite literally, their previous conceptions of their sense of self have faded away and been updated to account for a more present version, unrestricted by previously hardwired thoughts about who they were.

And ego dissolution is not restricted to just psychedelics; after all, the entire goal of most "mindfulness meditation" ceremonies is to achieve the same effect without the influence of external substances. In many studies, they found that, just like LSD, key nodes of the DMN had reportedly decrease in activity.[96] However, these were highly experienced mediators with nearly fourteen to sixteen years of experience, "including daily practice and retreats"![97] A non-experienced mediator had nowhere near this level of DMN inhibition, if at all.

And in the long-term, when it comes to other psychedelics, another group of researchers led by Calvin Ly at the University of California "*demonstrated that psychedelic compounds such as LSD, DMT, and DOI increase dendritic arbor complexity, promote dendritic spine growth, and stimulate synapse formation.*"

In English, this means *"psychedelics promote structural and functional neural plasticity".*[98] This also makes sense because, as we saw in Chapter 1, after just one psychedelic experience, we observed that OCEAN personality traits were changed, in which human desire to learn (O^+), be disciplined (C^+), and connect with others (E^+) significantly increases, while mental instability (N^-) decreases.

Finally, we can also see that no traditional psychedelics, LSD, psilocybin, mescaline or DMT, have resulted in fatalities.[99] So rest assured, when psychedelics are consumed responsibly, we're not pumping our veins full of toxic substances that can cause our arteries to burst or fry the human brain.

Instead, the harms of psychedelics are very different from the ones most people are familiar with when it comes to alcohol, cocaine, or opioids. Instead, psychedelics are among one of the most physiologically safe drugs we humans can consume. However, as we'll find out in Part III, Mind Leap, to ensure the safe use of these substances, we will explore how each frame of mind that psychedelics can induce have a very different list of precautions.

With all this information now available to us, it is time to find out what we can do with all the unique abilities that psychedelics offer the human mind, and how tapping into the unconscious lower levels of our brain can aid 'humans' global prosperity in a variety of ways.

The next part will be broken into four rapid-fire Chapters, filled with conceptual tools on how we can use the psychedelic experience to achieve a Mind Leap.

MIND LEAP

The first frame of mind is called **healing minds**, which discusses how tapping into this unconscious network of thinking can help solve the contagious problem of rising mood disorders within the twenty-first century. In addition, this frame of mind will discuss how humans can break out of one the most common, *yet unmentioned*, syndromes that affect many, without even knowing.

For now, think of this frame of mind as one that aims to heal the *materialist contents* of reality or things within a degree of control. Things like your career, your familial relationships, daily habits, and past traumas fall within this mind's jurisdiction. While these concepts themselves are intangible because you can't hold a habit or a relationship in your hand, all these fields require your physical presence.

The second frame of mind is called the **productivity mind**, which details how business executives, content creators, and big thinkers have used them to increase productivity, insight, and well-being about the state of the world. We'll get to the bottom of why tech superstars like Steve Jobs and Bill Gates have reportedly used LSD, and why the now well-known concept, microdosing, as made famous by James Fadiman in his book, *"The Psychedelic Explorer's Guide"*, has taken a firm root in hyper-productive tech societies like Silicon Valley.

Perhaps these workaholic Silicon Valleyers are looking to find a better alternative to Adderall, replacing it with psychedelics as a smart-drug or performance enhancer. But what's the truth? At small doses, can humans tap into their unconscious lower levels of Thoughtware effectively?

The third frame of mind is known as the **research mind**, in which we unveil how a higher processing power of humans' sensory and visual perception might aid the breakthrough studies in science. In addition, how psychedelics can help academics venture out of their studious rabbit holes of thought, in which only individuals who speak the same modern language can understand them.

The research mind builds the fundamental framework in which humans grow their vast knowledge about their world, and how rethinking the mechanics behind education may alleviate the growing concerns of students spending more and more time at school to learn the intricate details that come with the generational software of the modern era.

Finally, our Mind Leap journey ends with **mystical minds**. While healing minds deal with the tangible components of reality, the mystical mind dives into the boundlessness of abstract thought and symbolic generation. This mindset deals with the language of order at a higher-minded level, in which its goal is to conceptualize imagined orders and govern individuals to ensure the prosperity not only of an individual's immediate community but also the global one.

Mystical minds are one of the most common ways to use psychedelics, as early shamans become vessels to channel their unconscious network of thinking and describe to their community how it might operate more effectively.

* * *

- **Healing Mind** – A frame of mind focused on enhancing individuality and mental resiliency.

- **Productive Mind** – A frame of mind focused on enhancing cooperation and creativity.

- **Mystical Mind** – A frame of mind focused on enhancing **enlightenment** and **spirituality**.

PART III

MIND LEAP

As we navigated through humanity's ancient history on the first wave of the psychedelic roller coaster, conceptualized the effects of cultural malware in the second wave, and discussed the routes humanity can achieve a Mind Leap in the third wave, we will now navigate how humans can use these substances effectively.

Because each frame of mind has vastly different thinking styles, we will discuss a few parameters during the next four Chapters.

In other words, the effectivity of these psychedelics frames of mind are primarily influenced by **Environmental, Cultural, and Chemical Reprogramming**

In general, we can conceptualize these three factors with the following definitions:

- **Environmental Reprogramming** is a protocol that molds the lower levels of human Thoughtware from the external pressures that come from our society and geography. Things like technology and climate fall into this category.

- **Cultural Reprogramming** is a protocol that molds our upper levels of human Thoughtware from the internal pressures that circulate within our society. Things like social norms and ingroup biases fall into this category

- **Chemical Reprogramming** is a protocol that molds our entire hierarchy of Thoughtware by consuming a distinct psychedelic substance at a specific dose. Things like taking LSD at one hundred vs 10 micrograms, or the difference between taking MDMA vs. psilocybin fall into this category.

CHAPTER 7

HEALING MINDS

—

Healing Mind—A frame of mind focused on enhancing **individuality** and **mental resiliency.**

When it comes to the healing frame of mind, the general goal is to adjust an individual's Thoughtware and enhance their ability to form **deeper relationships** with **Nature,** their **Community,** their **Work,** and, most importantly, **Ourselves.**

These fundamental traits initiate a sense of connection, motivation, and purpose in human life. But without them, we descend into frames of mind associated with alienation, as Karl Marx expressed during the birth of exponential societies in the industrial era of the mid-nineteenth century.

While Marx's economic ideas may be wildly controversial (*since they were used to construct the first communistic reigns of terror in China and Russia*), his social ideas strike a point of truth when he states:

"*The less you eat, drink and read books;*

the less you go to the theatre, the dance hall, the public house;

the less you think, love, theorize, sing, paint, fence, etc.,

the more you save-the greater becomes your treasure which neither moths nor dust will devour-your capital.

The less you are, the more you have; the less you express your own life, the greater is your alienated life-the greater is the store of your estranged being."

He's describing how society influences people, not by allowing them to manifest their own destiny but to manifest a society's destiny. Decisions are not chosen by the individual, they are chosen by the social and political climate of the collective. A society doesn't need a million artists; instead, they need a million construction workers to build hyper-productive manufacturing facilities. In turn, people and communities are disconnected as less time is spent doing the things they love, while they carry on with a role that society needs. And as time passes, perhaps the need to escape from reality and retreat into nature for a while pops up in the mind, and nature is also being torn down to produce an economic surplus.

In turn, while a society is exponentially growing, and the wealth of insights and innovative technologies skyrocket, the ability to find our place in the world has become over-encumbered by the sheer weight of materialistic goods.

We live in a society that measures happiness, not based on connection or well-being, but by an arbitrary metric of wealth, more commonly known as gross domestic product (GDP). But this is just a faulty metric.

For example, we see an explosion of the Korean economy after 1987, nearly a 200 percent increase in its GDP rate, when **"labor emerged as a major political force, and rising wages gave further impetus to the development of more capital-intensive industry"**.[100, 101]

And from the newly erected infrastructure and job allocation, Korea saw an unprecedented quantity of innovative technologies pushed to the surface of their economy. Humanoid robots, mobile television, digital refrigerators, and the list goes on and on, as Korean societies jumped on the boat of the global technology arms race.

They were making more money than ever before, and as we know, a high GDP equals greater happiness, right? This might be true for the collective society; however, isolating members that form this collection, we arrive at an astounding conclusion about Korea.

"Over the last fifty years, Korea has undergone unprecedented economic growth and changes in social values. As a result, mental health problems have become a national issue. **Korea has the second-highest suicide mortality rate** (25.8 per one hundred,000 population)".[102]

While many factors could have led to this result, GDP is not necessarily indicative of mental well-being. And I won't make the claim that every person should quit their jobs and pursue their deepest desires to become artists, dancers, or YouTubers—or get their pitchforks and torches out to protest the totalitarian pressures of society. That's just nonsense.

But we can reconceptualize our roles in society and see how we can benefit the collective while also maintaining mental fortitude and resilience. In other words, we must be realistic about our desires, but at the same time, we shouldn't be afraid to push the borders beyond what our roles in society entitle.

But obviously this is much easier said than done.

So, why does it feel challenging to push past these borders?

What features of the modern era are pushing individuals into states in desperate need of a healing mind?

And for that matter, how can psychedelics serve as tools to help individuals achieve a healing mind?

CONSUMERISM

Modern society has molded the corporate working classes' minds into those representing robotic drones of productivity. After prolonged exposure to capitalistic structures and its fast-paced nature, many individuals eventually degrade the very language meant to reconstruct balance in an individual's life, the language of instinct.

Individuals gradually place less and less weight on their 'gut feeling' as they become ensnared in the vicious cycle of societal growth and mass-productivity. But it wasn't always like this.

For a good portion of human history, the most widely used language of order was theocracy, in which order was instilled with abstract concepts, subjective moral and ethical compasses, that assigned the value of a society. However, when using one of these compasses to understand which society was "best" when comparing to other theocracies, we realize this language of order proved subsequently less fruitful.

For example, early societies didn't get very far by saying their religion was better and enforcing it on others. Briefly detouring into ancient history, we can observe the violent tendencies that religion fueled as far back as 1500 BCE during the wars of Israel vs. Canaan, the Muslim conquests of 624 AD, and the more commonly known battle of the Crusades during the eleventh and twelfth centuries, and the list goes on and on. Meanwhile, human blood continues to spill out onto terrestrial grounds stained by religious superiority.

However, as currency and other inventions started fueling new forms of powerfully imagined orders like autocracies and democracies, people began to realize that technology itself became extremely effective tools to help quantify the value of a society.

With the invention of boats and ships, humans could expand their horizons and explore new ways to map out their physical landscape, while they could also be used to launch large-scale naval attacks, stealth missions to flank unsuspecting enemies—clearly, the value of this technology was inherent. On the other hand, while religious ideas might inspire individuals, without the proper technology or bank full of hard cash, the value of early theocracies seemed entirely too subjective. Who's to say one religion is better or more valuable than the other?

But, with the technology, the value metric is much more transparent. And it's obvious to us now that if asked, what's more valuable—one gold coin or two, what the right answer would be. So traditional imagined orders, like religion, faded away with the power of currency and revolutionary technology, and in return, a new imagined order had been constructed to fill the void of social guidance, **consumerism**.

In other words, consumerism is an imagined order concerned with **materialism**, an arbitrary metric that uses tangible entities to assign value. However, for many thousands of years, societies lacked the infrastructure to mass produce technology, and therefore the idea of consumerism had yet to catch on—at least until the beginning of the industrial revolution in 1760.

MATTER OVER MIND

With the introduction of mass manufacturing facilities brought on by the innovative energy transformers of the industrial revolution, like coal, steam and petroleum engines, the world saw a transformation unlike anything we've ever seen before—as the technology industry began its exponential growth. This was the dawn of the industrial era, when humans began looking for ways to build more effective societies with the aid of technology. And at long last, from the economic womb of hyper-competition, consumerism was born, and slowly but surely, it became the primary language of order.

But consumerism had an interesting effect on humans' **environmental software.** With the new value metric assigned to consumerist systems, for a large majority of humans, they became obsessed with possessing new technology, generating a plethora of wealth, and attaching their identity to what they owned more so than what they could create. For this reason, I fear humans are feeling more alienated than ever before because, as we transition into the digital era of the twenty-first century, its resulting technologies have only added fuel to the fire of mood-disorders present within many modern societies.

The technology of the twenty-first century is targeting a very different component of humans, their Thoughtware. As Cal Newport, author of *Deep Work*, states, *"For the first time in human history, we've created technology that makes it possible to banish every last moment of solitude from your life because now you have ubiquitous high-speed wireless internet and a super-computer in your pocket and there's big back-end algorithms that will feed up to you an optimized selection of nuggets at any moment."*

But there's more to the story when it comes to Newport's statement. The super-computers in our pockets are not necessarily the demonizing agents. On the contrary, we can use their superior computational and connective powers to surpass our own biological limits.

With digital technologies, we've made great leaps in academia by analyzing and predicting climate patterns. We've unveiled the structure of our own DNA by using computers in conjunction with technologies like X-Ray Crystallography. In business, we've automated many of the mundane tasks like file organization through digitalization.

On a personal level, we've connected with people living in an entirely different hemisphere, allowing global cooperation to leave our pipe dreams and enter reality.

In other words, technology is not a bad thing, nor is consumerism or capitalism for that matter. The problem with the technology of the digital era is that they have evolved to start receiving *big back-end algorithms that will feed up to you an optimized selection of nuggets at any moment.*

There's a deeper meaning behind the motives of these *big-back-end algorithms*, one that takes consumerism to a whole new level.

While one might think the primary product being sold in the digital era is the technology itself, it's really just the auction house. In other words, the algorithms Newport is talking about are not actually selling a tangible entity. For instance, we must ask, how are connective platforms inside the digital world free to use?

How are they making money?

To answer this question, we realize that the more time individuals spend online, the larger their digital footprint. And a larger digital footprint equals more data for these connective platforms to harvest. This is where the big bucks roll in because advertising and marketing agencies will pay top dollars to these companies to have their ads selectively target individuals browsing these social media websites.

So in order to make fat stacks of green, these *big-back-end algorithms* function like a digital mousetrap—to keep people surfing the web, so more and more data can be harvested so that advertising agencies continue paying them to flood human Thoughtware with personalized advertisements. In effect, human **attention** has become the primary commodity of the twenty-first century. As Newport says, there's not a single moment of *solitude* to spare.

And as the black market for human attention grows larger each day, our ability to focus on the infinite oasis of information that exists within our own bodies has been sold by multi-billion-dollar social media platforms like Instagram, Facebook, Twitter, LinkedIn, and who knows how many more…

That means no more time to tap into our unconscious languages of instinct, the language that tells us who we are and how we feel, and yet we've neglected our own biology in exchange for a shiny new piece of tech.

And with humans' attention now devoted to these pieces of tech, nearly all human interactions with the world are done through the electronic interphases of their smartphones and laptops. And this is the problem with the technology that comes from the digital era. Computers have become a key component of our environmental software, in which nearly all the sensory information we receive is emitted through various blue screens and binary 1s and 0s. In effect, computers have become the fourth structure of the human brain, creating the first generation of cyborgs.

In other words, while these devices can highly amplify our journey's through life by quickly contacting others in moments of worry, doing complex calculations when number punching grows exhausting and transmitting valuable reminders when our memories draw a blank, the problem comes when they're hooked up to the internet, where a mixture of malevolent and beneficial information lives.

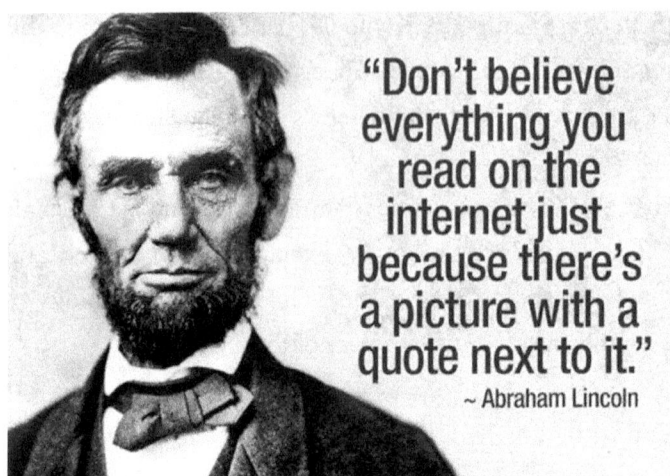

"Don't believe everything you read on the internet just because there's a picture with a quote next to it."
~ Abraham Lincoln

Image provided courtesy of the Internet.

But automatically, our brain associates the value that technology can provide as something beneficial, and so we gravitate toward trusting information on the internet when we don't have an argument to provide. Without extensive knowledge about a subject matter, it's easy to fall into the trap of cultural malware, as we saw during the second wave of the psychedelic revolution, when blind faith was assigned to the many mass media programs that popped up on our home televisions. And since psychedelics were relatively new to American culture, no one questioned the authority of the mainstream media.

And as the potential in technology grows stronger than ever before, so, too, does the amount of trust we place in it. In effect, technology has started to take over the structures of the brain that control low-level Thoughtware thinking like "gut feelings". Instead of trusting the valuable insights that course within human Thoughtware, many individuals have become dependent on the vast computational power of their iPhones or laptops. On the internet, if they don't like something, they can just scroll to the next link and find something that fits into their conformational or ingroup biases quite nicely.

And when they're thrust into face-to-face interactions, instead of trying to understand others, they'll retreat, because they'll realize when a disagreement starts to form, they can't just discard and replace others with those that agree with them like they can on the internet. In effect, these individuals are gradually spending more and more time engaging in social activities through the lens of a blue screen, where they can sit back and relax as they spend every waking hour creating and interpreting entirely artificial versions of themselves and others.

However, in the process, their identity has now become defined by a digital medium of information, not a biological one. So they start to trust the notifications they receive on the internet more than their own biological ones, and in conjunction with large tech companies' digital mousetraps, they find their eyes glued to their digital screens.

This type of abuse, on both the individual and consumeristic side, has degraded our communicatory abilities.

For this reason, the healing mind is an essential component for humanity to achieve a Mind Leap. This state of mind promotes individuality and mental resiliency in a world selling human attention and disguising the truth from our eyes.

NON-PLAYER CHARACTER
SYNDROME (NPC-SYNDROME)

There's a reason why people like Simon Sinek, author of *Start With Why*, proclaim, *"In a Facebook-Instagram world (in other words we're good at putting filters on things)", "What we're seeing is as [Millennials"],"* a type of generational software, *"grow older, too many kids don't know how to form deep meaningful relationships, their words, not mine.*

*They will admit that many of their friendships are superficial. They will admit that they don't count on their friends, but they also know that their friends will cancel on them when something better comes along. **Deep meaningful relationships are not there"*.[103]

Individuals with this version of generational software have grown up in a world incentivized by materialism, one run on quantitative metrics like how much money or, more relevantly, how many Facebook friends or Instagram followers they have.

The twenty-first century is a world that uses GDP to classify the wealth of emotions an individual should be experiencing.

Instead of relying on **deep meaningful relationships** to deal with the many mental turmoils that humans experience throughout the course of their lives, they will rely on the products of materialism, things like social media, alcohol, or prescription medication to cope with their problems.

These entities are dopaminergic, and we know from Chapter 2 that much of the underlying phenomenon of human motivation is based on consuming substances that increase the concentration of dopamine in our bloodstream. It gives us a short burst of pleasure and briefly suppresses our fear (*more on this later*). And the interesting thing is that dopamine is also released when using technology, specifically social media (*which is probably another reason we've formed such an intimate relationship with these emotionless devices*).

"According to an article by Harvard University researcher Trevor Haynes, when you get a social media notification, your brain sends dopamine along a reward pathway," reprogramming human Thoughtware to seek social media outlets as a source of pleasure. But our human brains didn't evolve that way.[104, 105]

On a neurological level, we realized that dopamine is a neurotransmitter generally associated with reward when humans accomplish a beneficial task like sex and eating, which reinforces the desire to produce offspring and consume foods—tasks necessary to ensure the survival of a species.

Throughout humans' evolutionary history, the internet and social media are unique to humans' current version of generational software. In other words, the technologies of the digital revolution were not included in humans' neurological equation, and so we can realize that the threats imposed by digital technology have never been dealt with before. Many statements like those made by Sinek that describe the harms of digital technology have become ever-present in the modern era.

We're seeing a disconnection of human Thoughtware and its mental hardware. Because dopamine is released when we receive a text message or a new online friend request, it feels *fantastic* to use technology. "Look at how many connections, how many likes, or how much stuff I have" are the new phrases that echo throughout the chambers of materialistic societies.

Rarely do individuals stop and think about what mental abilities they're losing when they become engrossed in their technological abilities. Simply put, they start neglecting signals of their body, "gut feelings" that tell us who our true friends are and what emotional states we occupy. As mentioned previously, the powers of the human mind shine during face-to-face interactions, direct confrontations with the world. When it comes to making *deep relationships* in a world littered with edited body language on online platforms and handpicked images that only reveal humans at their *best*, many individuals start to jump on board the bandwagon of media abuse.

In effect, the very lines of code that allow these individuals to speak the language of instinct are gradually becoming forgotten. In return, as we lose the ability to communicate introspectively, the languages necessary to form *deep meaningful relationships* follow suit.

And neurologically, this checks out too. Of the vast array of neurons that make up humans' mental hardware, some of which are known as **mirror neurons**. These neurons fire *"when an animal acts and when the animal observes the same action performed by another".* While the exact reason these types of neurons evolved in animals is still under much debate, when we see others engage in an activity, chances are we'll follow—hence the term "monkey see, monkey do".[106]

When we observe behavior through internet mediums, in which individuals are generating hand-picked versions of themselves, we'll follow suit. With all these factors considered, we finally arrive at one of the root causes behind why people don't know themselves, and subsequently, why the current version of generational software is struggling to forge deeper relationships.

By placing more trust in the reality that technology portrays, many individuals have started to lose trust in themselves and their own internal language. In other words, the innate ability to tap into the unconscious lower levels of Thoughtware has started to dissolve. In return, as time passes and the barrier between the lower and higher levels of Thoughtware grows in strength, the resulting cultural software becomes a **mirror** image of other perceptions not their own.

Therefore, trying to obtain a Mind Leap is out of the question. These individuals must make sure shifting their frame of mind lies in bounds with their reprogrammed cultural software, other thoughts, not their own.

In effect, I might argue that the reason we often feel restricted from obtaining a new frame of mind is a product of something called **Non-Player Character-Syndrome, or NPC-Syndrome**. This syndrome arises from a lack of individuality, a Thoughtware protocol that obscures desires and sacrifices them for those embedded within a collective's cultural software. For those who've played role-playing games, NPCs might be more closely associated with the characters in a video game that do and say things repeatedly, like a broken record, every time they're approached.

In video games, NPCs do not choose their role—they are placed in a role handpicked by video game developers to fit within the boundaries of the game. For example, an NPC might take the form of a shopkeeper, in which they'll wear the game's stereotypical '*shopkeeper*' outfit. They'll know the game's jargon, be up to date with the latest in-game news and events, and the only role they play the game is when they say, "That'll be X dollars and Y cents," every time a transaction is made. At the peak of their curiosity, they might even ask someone, "How's the weather outside" or "How are you doing today?"

They arrive at the shop and leave at the same time, of course, making sure to get home with enough time for their in-game family and, after supper, they might be caught messing around with entertainment systems unique to the video game.

In other words, the life of an NPC is predictable, stagnant, which makes it easy for gamers to interact with them, but the sad truth is that I feel that NPC-Syndrome is a very relatable phenomenon in the real world. For the most part, we'd expect children to say they want to become "the president" or "an astronaut" when they grow up, not an NPC; that's just inhumane.

While my argument is not necessarily literal, *people aren't that simple,* without being able to tap into the lower levels of human Thoughtware, just like the video game programmers that encode NPCs, people become no different as their society encodes them. What's the difference?

NPC-Syndrome is the product of being hand-fed individually crafted advertisements, personalized career suggestions, online friend requests, and many more. It's a human's desire to quantify human biology (again, not necessarily bad), stimulating the growth of NPC-Syndrome.

If caught with a serious case of NPC-Syndrome, computers will decide what you think you decide to do. NPC-Syndrome got you down, take these antidepressant medications that will treat your symptoms. Don't like your job, sign up for one of the newest, most innovative, job search platforms that will cater to all your ambitions. And then you move locations, get settled into a new environment fit with a full prescription of antidepressants, and everything is great. But then you realize that you just moved locations and went from punching a bunch of numbers at location A to punching a bunch of numbers at location B.

However, along the way, your NPC-Syndrome was never treated because it would require an entire society to change. Luckily, the third wave of the psychedelic revolution is upon us, fit with a few solutions that might aid us in our shifting our frames of mind, so as not to get lost in the boundlessness of NPC-Syndrome.

PSYCHEDELIC THERAPY

The most important thing to realize about NPC-Syndrome is that it's not necessarily stimulating the growth of mood-disorders in society. On the contrary, NPC-Syndrome is a rather comfortable state of mind. Life moves at a steady rate, while days and weeks become months and years of complacent routine. There's no need to overexert the mind, just being present in the world is good enough.

However, when a mood-disorder does start to take form, either through job or relationship dissatisfaction–causing **depression** or **worthlessness**, a traumatic experience—causing **PTSD** or **substance abuse**, or a sudden mid-life crisis—causing **mental fatigue** or **anxiety**, a serious case of NPC-Syndrome disables the human mind from changing their behavioral patterns and habits—frames of mind that can help individuals revisit the core elements that underlie their disorderly emotional states.

And because the digital era's version of consumerism incentivizes the use of technology through digital media, to support advertising campaigns or online shopping, to keep the flow of wealth alive, the need for individuality has become lost, catalyzing the development of NPC-Syndrome. Instead, NPCs will cope, not by engaging in solitude to repair their mental damage once and for all, rather they will rely on the pleasureful, numbing effects that come with dopamine every time they open up their phones and receive a notification or purchase a new item that marginally improves their day-to-day lives.

In other words, the consumerist practices embedded within the digital era, have obscured many individuals' ability to open the doors that contain valuable insights about their present sense of self. Instead, fear of change filters through the NPC-like mind because NPC-Syndrome is a frame of mind that embraces comfort above all else.

In turn, we can finally answer the first way we can use psychedelics' unique properties (*discussed in Chapter 6*) to achieve a healing mind. In this case, the first psychedelic we stumble upon is MDMA, *at 200mg*, which might disable more severe cases of NPC-Syndrome. MDMA has some very interesting features that distinguish it from other psychedelics, like LSD or psilocybin.

When I spoke with Dr. Ben Sessa, a psychotherapist at Mandala Therapy Limited, he told me:

"I've become quite disillusioned with the current, traditional psychiatric method, namely the medications we tend to use are maintenance medications that only treat the overlying symptoms, but don't treat the underlying cause. And the psychotherapy we use are good, but many patients **find it hard to engage** with psychotherapy and complete psychotherapy courses because they are so **overwhelmed by the negative** aspect that goes with the **call of trauma** that **they can't engage** and complete psychotherapy.

In other words, A: The drugs are inefficient and don't work, and B: the psychotherapies are inefficient and don't work because people can't engage with the core reason why they're unwell.

So psychedelics and MDMA-assisted psychotherapy provide stable mental states which patients can use in combination with psychotherapy, to **finally address those core features that are driving their mental health problem, that they've not previously been able to engage with and reflect upon to challenge those results."**

In other words, MDMA isn't just the average run-of-the-mill drug; rather, its unique properties are associated with human fear.

For example, Sessa continues, "There's many drugs that inhibit the fear response, a bottle of vodka or a bag of heroin will effectively inhibit the fear response which is why these are popular drugs to control trauma." In addition, we can add in the fact that, just like social media, these drugs are ones that release dopamine, instantaneous bumps of pleasure that momentarily serve as an effective coping strategy.

However, they don't help individuals engage a healing mind to repair their mood-disorders. When they're consumed, "You're **cognitively impaired**, you **can't remember**, you **can't reflect**, you **can't debate**, and the next day you won't remember what you talked about on those drugs.

What's bizarre, in a really wonderful way, about MDMA, is its **ability to selectively inhibit fear. But all the other faculties are fine, you can remember and debate and reflect. And the next day, you remember everything you said.** So it's a very unique selective fear inhibition that makes MDMA so interesting."

What's also very interesting is that we realize that most substances, *like alcohol, opioids, and cocaine,* and social activities, like online networking, social media scrolling, and online shopping, are all primarily dopaminergic activities. These entities stimulate the reward pathway of the brain, and, therefore, humans' addictive tendencies and shallowness in thinking. In other words, NPC-behavior, fit with its inability to speak the language of instinct, might be a product of a society abusing dopamine. When dopamine is released in the human brain, it causes satisfaction, the desire to continue doing the same thing even if an activity is potentially harmful.

And from Dr. Sessa's conjecture in conjunction with the triune brain model we proposed previously, we can perhaps conclude that dopaminergic activities disable information from flowing from the lower evolutionary structures, the primal and emotional brain, into the higher evolutionary structure, the rational brain. When we observe individuals operating at **high dopaminergic states**, induced by alcohol or heroin in this case, their behavior is clearly most often categorized as irrational.

They become extremely **emotionally vulnerable**, impulsive animals that rarely produce high-minded thoughts, waving their arms about erratically, and, most often, ranting incomprehensibly. However, while it's easy to make interpretations on the surface, there is a fundamental reason why, when comparing MDMA and other psychedelics to these dopaminergic drugs, this results in a vastly different frame of mind.

By honing our attention to two specific components of our emotional brain, the masterminds behind an emotional regulation called the *Ventral Tegmentum (VTA)* and the *Amygdala*, we can tie up all the loose ends in this Chapter.

According to Andreas Komninos, a researcher at the Computer Technology Institute and adjunct professor at the Hellenic Open University, "The VTA contains dopaminergic neurons, which release dopamine when stimulated by sensory information." By using the dopamine, VTA can then become "responsible for **processing emotional output** from the amygdala," a structure in the brain "thought to play an integral in our **avoidance** and **fear response**".[107]

And for most people, while fear transmits valuable information when we're in danger, it's quite clearly not a preferable emotional state—hence why dopaminergic activities have been extremely popular in the modern era with binge drinking, binge social networking, and binge shopping. When dopamine-seeking behavior is continually reinforced and then, suddenly, becomes absent from the human brain, we crave it because not only does dopamine feel good, it also helps humans cope with their problems by inhibiting fear— hence the formation of addictive tendencies toward these activities. They all release dopamine!

However, psychedelics, predominantly release serotonin, or in the case of MDMA, serotonin, norepinephrine (the "alert" chemical messenger), and dopamine, descending in chemical stimulation, respectively.

Modern neuroscience tells us that serotonin produces **"hyper-synchronous discharges** that link" the primal and emotional brain together, allowing information to flow **unrestrictedly** through all three structures of the human brain. In other words, *as we observed in the fMRI scan of an LSD-induced patient in Chapter 6*, all components of the brain are hyperactive—these structures become electrically connected as information is sent from the unconscious into the conscious structures of the brain **harmoniously**. [108]

And because MDMA also stimulates dopamine activity, not only is the brain rewired to speak the language of instinct once again (*due to the linking between uncon-scious/conscious structures*) but also, the human fear response is inhibited.

In effect, after consuming MDMA inside a controlled environment, not a chaotic or hectic one like a music festival, individuals can leap into a healing mind. And with the addition of psychotherapy to lend a supportive hand as individuals explore the inner workings of their mind fearlessly, we see that MDMA psychotherapy has nearly doubled the effectivity of helping individuals repair their mood-disorders.

In other words, even after spending years descending further into NPC-Syndrome, individuals who consume MDMA have demonstrated that they're not necessarily more likely to develop a mood disorder. On the contrary, materialistic abuse has likely reprogrammed their Thoughtware. In turn, their ability to obtain a healing mind was simply restricted, not non-existent.

As more promising trials, *done by MAPS*, continue to breach public news, MDMA has been declared a **Breakthrough Therapy**, gaining phase 3 clinical approval by the FDA in 2019.[109]

And it doesn't stop there—the serotonergic properties of other psychedelics, like psilocybin, have also been breaking records to help individuals with addiction problems. For example, a study conducted at Johns Hopkins University tested fifteen individuals, ten men and five women, who were all mentally and physically healthy. Yet, on average, *they smoked nineteen cigarettes a day for thirty-one years and had repeatedly tried and failed to stop smoking.*

So in order to get them to stop smoking once and for all, Matthew W. Johnson, the lead researcher of this study, administered two to three high doses (20mg and 30mg/70kg) of psilocybin. Their results found an "**80 percent abstinence rate** over six months, compared to an approximate **35 percent success rate** for patients taking varenicline, which is widely considered to be the most effective smoking cessation drug".[110]

And if psychedelics can allow people to develop a deeper relationship with themselves and their own problems, who knows, it might even strengthen their relationships with others in a world dominated by technological disconnection. I'll leave this to speculation, mainly because no evidence exists for or against this idea in modern scientific literature.

However, it's important to emphasize that, with the unique features that come with these serotonergic drugs, they can be used in a multitude of ways, as we'll find out in later Chapters. In other words, the drugs aren't the healing devices; they're just tools to help individuals shift into a healing mind. **The mind itself is the healing tool.**

Johnson stresses, "**When administered after careful preparation and in a therapeutic context**, psilocybin can lead to deep reflection about one's life and spark motivation to change." On the other hand, without being cognizant of our environmental software (the influences of our surroundings) at high doses, **psychedelics can be misused** and transpire individuals into a malevolent Thoughtware.

"Use them with care and use them with respect as to the transformations they can achieve, and you have an extraordinary research tool.

Go banging about with a psychedelic drug for a Saturday night turn-on, and you can get into a really bad place, psychologically.

Know what you're using, decide just why you're using it, and you can have a rich experience. They're not addictive, and they're certainly not escapist, either, but they're exceptionally valuable tools for understanding the human mind, and how it works."

– ALEXANDER SHULGIN

* * *

Finally, I want to address a question in this Chapter that has yet to be answered:

What defines a **mentally healthy society**—a **dopaminergic** (*focusing more on dopamine stimulation*) or a **serotonergic** (*focusing more on serotonin stimulation*) one?

CHAPTER 8

PRODUCTIVE MINDS

———

- **Productive Mind** – A frame of mind focused on enhancing an individual's cognitive creativity and visionary capabilities.

Productivity is an interesting feature of the human condition. Quite simply, the human-animal is the only creature on Earth that has become obsessed with mass producing and manipulating the many core features of our planet. And even when we map out the historical topography that defines the evolution of our species, we categorize previous eras based on the technology and ideas that sailed out of human imagination and arrived on the shores of reality.

From the collapse of the rocky stone age,

past the smoky forges of the bronze and iron age,

the marble jungles of ancient Roman architecture,

the theological and artistic explosions of the middle ages,

the coal-burning generators and black gold mines of the pre and post-industrial era,

and finally, to the electrical circuits and computational algorithms of the digital era,

humanity has been hard at work, for who knows how many thousands of years–embracing the core values of consumerism, transforming abstract ideas into concrete products.

These concrete products, whether they take the form of tangible objects, like a cellphone or a car, or a string of ideas that morphs a collection of words into a book or an array of colors into a painting, are all ways to analyze and store information about the world long after our last breaths.

By nature, the human-animal is a creative genius, built in such a way that enables adept hand-eye coordination and motor dexterity, fit with a huge neo-cortex, *that we called the rational brain in previous Chapters*, capable of interpreting and synthesizing abstract ideas and imagined orders, like transformative visions that inspire or governing systems that provide trust and safety.

But, there's just one problem when it comes to producing both products and ideas in the modern era. Even though the human-animal has the potential to innovate and has an extremely malleable Thoughtware, many individuals have fallen into a trap thinking that productivity is just a *number's* game. Today, questions beginning with **how much** or **how many** dominate employee productivity assessment. In other words, the reliance on dehumanizing metrics to define productivity has become all to present within working environments.

In the process, it seems like we've forgotten how to evaluate work performance in both a supportive and less stressful way. So, to remind ourselves of what a productivity mind looks like in exponentially evolving societies, we'll set out to grapple with a few challenging questions in this chapter.

What are the defining components of frames of mind devoted to quantitative mind sets?

And what frame of mind might alleviate that crushing weight of stress that stands in the way of optimizing employee productivity?

Finally, how can psychedelics catapult individuals into this more effective state and unleash their own version of the productivity mind?

VALUE GAMES

According to James P. Carse, a theologian at New York University, *"There are at least two kinds of games—one could be called finite, the other infinite.*

A finite game is played for the purpose of winning, an infinite game for the purpose of continuing the play."

And depending on which type of game we're trying to play, our motives and actions become drastically than one another. Simply put, each game requires a different frame of mind to play. In turn, it must be that a productivity mind playing the finite game shares little features with the one playing the infinite game.

A finite game is one with agreed-upon rules, a clear start and finish line, and **known players**. They use a pre-defined metric, a scoreboard, to figure out who wins the game once it's over. For example, sports like football, chess, or online gaming are types of finite games. A football, chess, or video game player knows the rules, who he's playing against, and what factors decide when the game ends. And when two finite players are pitted against one another, the system is stable because they both agree that only one person can win.

Finite games take on many forms, like when competing for different job positions or on a much larger scale, when two nations are at war to claim a region or a territory, but in both cases, only one of the players will take the spot. In other words, all finite players care about is the **outcome**.

On the other hand, in an infinite game, there are no rules, no scoreboard, no winning, and it consists of both **known** and **unknown players**. For example, life, in totality, is playing this game. It uses natural selection to progress, as the pressures of the environment inadvertently shape how this evolution mechanic works. In this case, the species of life are the known players, while the stimuli that arise from the environment are the unknown players.

But life doesn't care about the outcome because there is no set time limit. Its only aim is to keep the evolutionary cycle in play. And from a human's perspective, when they decide to produce offspring, a species can keep playing the infinite game. The players don't care about the outcome; rather, the infinite game is outcome-less. When two infinite players are pitted against one another, the system is also stable.

In other words, finite games are derived from metrics and quantities, while infinite games are derived from purposes and visions.

When a finite player is pitted against an infinite player, the whole system destabilizes.

For example, a relationship with a friend or a loved one can be thought of as a type of infinite game. As humans, it's obvious a relationship is not won—it's earned. That's why buying friends is a rather worthless activity, there's no trust, no deeper purpose or vision that keeps the friendship alive.

All too often, we seem to think using the metrics and rules that come with finite to describe human productivity is something different, as if we suddenly win a higher state of productivity if we can produce more stuff or work longer hours at work. But this is a delusion brought on by the players of finite games. In turn, the many problems we're seeing in the digital era stem from using productive minds that succeeded in finite games only to fail or become exhausted when playing infinite games.

FINITE MINDS

The daily 9 to 5 job during the manufacturing era of the early twentieth century was a simple process. People knew exactly what a productive mind looked like on a day-to-day basis. If they contacted X amount of people, accelerated Y products into the development pipeline, or generated Z amount of commission, people would go home feeling like they had engaged their productive mind. They were all finite games, easily quantifiable with set parameters and a clear vision that told people what productivity looked like.

However, as technology and science became exponentiated in progress, workloads become ever-increasing as we suddenly transitioned into the infantile stages of the digital era during the late twentieth century. The simple jobs of the twentieth century, like assembly workers and retail clerics, were replaced by stationary robots and online shopping. And for a good majority, many feared that automation was synonymous with job replacement. But they feared automation for the wrong reasons.

The real fear is that "Our world has become ever more cognitively challenging. A hundred years ago, nearly one-third of Americans lived on a farm; today that figure is less than 2 percent. Only in the 1920s did radio become popular; not until the late 1950s did television reach most homes; as recently as the year 2000 fewer than half of all U.S. homes had access to the internet; the smart-phone as we know it didn't exist until Apple released the iPhone in 2007. "We are the first of our species to live in a world dominated by categories, hypotheticals, nonverbal symbols, and visual images that paint alternative realities," Flynn has written. "We have evolved to deal with a world that would have been alien to previous generations."

The bright-eyed curiosity of an average twenty-something year old, fresh out of college and ready to shock the world with their profound **finite game teachings**, presents a brilliantly horrid metamorphosis.

They're suddenly launched into a world that can mass-produce technology at the drop of a hat. And as soon as they learn the inner workings of their new company and start to get comfortable, the latest and greatest advancements in the industry breeches headlines.

Moments later, their boss tells them to discard what they just learned, because what's been learned is already outdated. It's no wonder the accumulation of electronic waste is starting to breach 50 million tons. That's the metric equivalent of throwing out a spaceship each year!

If this company doesn't do a major technology overhaul, not only will the individual find themselves out of a job, but the company will burn through their resources trying to stay afloat with their now-primitive technology.

In turn, these individuals realize capitalistic culture has become a competitive beast, the *biggest and baddest* player of the twenty-first century's most celebrated economic game of materialism.

And the biggest delusion is that they think there will be an end to the game. But the finite games of the industrial era have evolved into the infinite game of the digital era. There's no winning anymore, and if employees aren't willing to constantly reinvent themselves, they'll find themselves losing steam in the exponential maze of learning new skills, only to discard them when the next round of exponential technology surfaces. And quite frankly—it's extremely exhausting! Many individuals just aren't willing to take on the tremendous stress that comes with ever-changing job market.

Take for example two different players of the twenty-first century's retail industry, Toys R Us, a finite player, and Amazon, an infinite player. When Toys R Us was founded in the 1950s, it was a dream-like wonderland for the average pre-adolescent—they could run through the store isles, filled with vast collections of colorful toys, and feel more materialistic joy than ever before. However, when Amazon came along, suddenly the twentieth century's rules for retail sales had transformed. Technology enabled children to scroll through an even more expansive online retail store, a seemingly infinite wormhole of toy-heaven.

This is exactly why in September 2017, the seventy-year-old retailer, Toys R Us, filed for bankruptcy. They were trying to sell **toys**, while Amazon was trying to sell **everything**.[111] There was just no competition. Marginally better toys could never keep up with Amazon's superior selection and accessibility. A finite player will never beat an infinite one.

Capitalist culture is now playing an infinite game. There's just one problem; in the infinite game, where survival is everything, many companies are still using the age-old metric of productivity brought on by the twentieth century. The reason corporate giants like Amazon or Microsoft are still so successful is that they're burning through human productivity like there's no tomorrow.

The disappointing reality for most corporations is that people aren't just sponges that can be squeezed for every ounce of their productivity. On the contrary, what shifts people into a more productive state of mind are the warm and fuzzy connections between people over the cold and rigid ones with money. However, while *89 percent of bosses believe employees quit because they want more money, only 12 percent of employees actually leave an organization for more money"*.[112] In other words, the problem here lies within prioritizing economic gain over empathetic gain.

Take, for example, a statistic calculated by the Bureau of Labor Statistics, which found that the ratio of managers to employees was 1:19. That means that of the nineteen non-manager employees, only one will get promoted, so what happens to the other eighteen? In an ideal workplace with empathetic priorities, they will stay because, while the promoted role makes more money, employees still find **value in the internal connections** they've made within the company.[113] In other words, what's important in the infinite game is not internal competition—it's internal cooperation. It's all about the purpose that a company's culture instills in its people.

In a finite company, a **boss** wants to **pay for results**, while an **employee** wants **recognition for their effort**. Without recognition, or a cooperative environment, the productivity mind of an employee is locked away, and in effect, according to the World Health Organization (WHO), workplace '**burn-out**' has become a legitimate syndrome in 2019. The International Classification of Diseases (IDC) has also officially listed 'burn-out' in their manual, not as a medical issue, but as an **occupational issue**.[114]

If a company clings on to the age-old practices of the industrial era's finite games, defined by over incentivizing **marginal gains** in a company, the overwhelming weight of surviving in an infinite game with finite rules will crush what once was a firm foundation to grow. So these individuals will quit when they stop getting recognition or when the company's culture is all about product development instead of an underlying vision to unify its employees.

"Gallup estimates that Millennial turnover costs the U.S. economy $30.5 billion annually." It's not just millennials either. "The median tenure of the workforce's most senior workers declined from 1983 to 2006 and has slowly increased through 2016".[115]

Clearly, something is very wrong with how many companies are understanding worker productivity. Therefore, in the most competitive work environments in the world, people are flocking to psychedelics to help them fix the problem.

MICRODOSING

The now-well-known concept, microdosing, as made famous by James Fadiman in his book, "The *Psychedelic Explorer's Guide*", has taken a firm root in hyper-productive tech societies like Silicon Valley. Perhaps these workaholic, burn-out prone Silicon Valleyers' are looking to find a better alternative to Adderall, replacing it with psychedelics as a smart-drug or productivity enhancer. The theory with this approach is that we can manipulate human Thoughtware by introducing a trace amount of a psychedelic.

At 1/10 of the recreational dose, psychedelics operate 'sub-perceptually,' meaning that many of the commonly reported hallucinogenic effects become suppressed. In return, micro-dosing then allows the user to experience a state of consciousness claimed to boost creativity and mental well-being without inducing the dissociative state of mind associated with recreational tripping.

So seeking a way to alleviate the over-encompassing feelings of job-burnout, psychedelics have become a huge hit in the tech industry. And among the large list of psychedelics, LSD has roared with overwhelming popularity in this region. LSD has an average duration of eight hours, nearly the same amount of time spent at work. Taken before entering the workplace, a user can experience LSD's effect throughout the entire day. On the other hand, those just looking for a morning psychedelic boost might opt for psilocybin mushrooms. It's only active in the human brain for half the time.

In other words, taken at these sub-perceptual doses these drugs enable the user just to slightly alter their cognitive perception while simultaneously reducing their stress levels. For people looking to increase their innovative output, or simply reduce the amount of pressure experienced throughout the day, the micro-dosing tactic has reportedly seen overwhelmingly positive results.

It's interesting that research done in 2019 found that on micro-dosing days, people reported feeling more connected, contemplative, creative focused, happy, productive, and well. However, *"these findings indicate that microdosing led to general increases in psychological functioning rather than specific effects"*.[117] In other words, by slightly boosting the power out of humans' mental hardware, individuals have found it helps them connect with other individuals at a more personal level. In turn, this is catalyzing the positive emotions they feel in a work environment, decreasing anxiety, stress, and mind-wandering, while increasing their mindfulness and their ability to cooperate.

One individual reported, "Microdosing has a *significant impact on my ability to get in touch with what is going on deep inside.* Although this is not always a pleasant experience, I have a strong feeling that psilocybin helps to reveal what I need to see in myself and the world."

Another, stated, "I had a very reflective day. I felt blissfully connected with nature and came up with optimistic ideas for the future."

But there are mixed emotions about microdosing in that some might say, "On a microdose, I sometimes feel weird or alien to myself and others. And another negative is that all emotions get amplified. So whenever I feel down or not loved, the microdose makes it even harder."

But the key thing is microdosing is an effective way to shift the mind, but it's not a technique to shift an individual's core personality, as we saw in the case of the healing mind. On the contrary, they're helping individuals **relearn** how to rebuild connections in a work environment, and of course, this can be both an enlightening and uncomfortable experience, as we've observed.

But this is the beauty of these serotonergic chemicals. They are polar-opposites of the one-track, solitude-minded effects of dopaminergic chemicals like caffeine or nicotine.

And as more companies are starting to queue up into the infinite games of modern capitalism, these serotonergic effects boost productivity. I might argue that dopaminergic chemicals are great for finite games since, quite literally, dopamine is concerned with short-term victories and rewards, while serotonergic chemicals are great for infinite games— concerned with sustainability and emotional realization.

Therefore, the productive mind induced by psychedelics will not help an individual increase their output, but rather their quality—which is an essential feature of a world looking to gain stability. Psychedelics are not grunt tools, they're not to be binged, and they're surely not to be used to play finite games. Microdosing is just one way to shift the cognitive playing field to incentivize humanism, cooperation, over roboticism, competition.

CHAPTER 9

MYSTICAL MINDS

———

Mystical Mind – A frame of mind focused on enhancing **enlightenment** and **spirituality**.

The language of order is the most unifying language of the human species—it is a powerful abstract framework that takes the form of nations, governments, and religions. The habitual mechanisms that underlie our own Thoughtware are mandated by these languages. In this sense, this is a type of mind unlike both the healing and productive water-scarce, in that the only goal is to explore these languages of order—to navigate through our own unique frames of Thoughtware and understand what types of thinking styles can remove the overarching threats of nihilism and replace it with a sense of meaning.

In other words, this is a frame of mind not to help us navigate through our lives in the material world but, rather, to help us understand the human consciousness itself from the lens of spirituality. What is this mysterious creature that motivates our actions and desires, and on a deeper level, why are languages of order necessary in the first place?

A HUMAN EXPERIENCE

Many of us have heard of the archetypal story of someone stranded in the desert. Lost in a sandy oasis, struggling to force down gulps of air in wake of dehydration, a human might find themselves creating their own mental imagery. Under extreme stress, the human mind reacts chaotically, constructing alternate versions of reality to soothe their desperate emotional state. Those who live to tell their story speak of vast golden empires like El Dorado peaking over the mountain crests and tropical landscapes filled with fairies and nymphs, yet humanity has never collected legit evidence on any of these claims.

The interesting thing is that humans don't need a desert to imagine a fantasy world–our dreams and fantasies are constantly taking roots in our minds. The only difference is that we don't fully believe in most of the stories we tell ourselves. However, cast away in water-scarce environments, we become desperate to believe in something, even if we must make it up.

And this is the major dilemma that the mystical mind aims to solve—this type of mind that helps us verify our own perceptions and construct order in a world of chaos.

For example, an individual's emotions can generate unadulterated desires to indulge in the labors of nature. A stimulus that allowed a person to experience joy can be misleading and motivate the user to constantly use that stimuli. In other words, **what was once good isn't always good. Stimuli assessment should be made conditionally, case by case, not absolutely.** While a human might find it constructive to over-consume to increase the short-term quality of life, in the long-term, the source of production may be exhausted and the human will be left to decay in wake of its parasitic tendencies to indulge. If an individual falls prey to absolutes, it can transform a person's life into a self-consuming cycle of destruction. Therefore, consumption without restraint can become self-destructive. But without a centralizing form of discipline, this concept is not intuitive.

Perhaps this is the true insight humanity's ancestors were referencing when they glorified psychedelic-producing plants and why the mystical mind was a crucial component of their cultures. They may have been aware of the innately irrational intent to over-consume and therefore sought ways in which they could suppress their emotions and build models of thought removed from personal subjectivity, in other words, **languages of order.**

To change the habits of a society, they became aware that, before manipulating a large mass of people, they must first tame the individual. Therefore, spirituality in this context is an individualistic phenomenon with two components—first engaging a healing mind, then a mystical mind. Upon doing so, traditional cultures could then build a cooperative system in which each member would understand their position within the community itself.

This is where psychedelics reveal their utility when using the mystical mind to build the first forms of religion. Religion serves as the fundamental framework which people could use to develop more certainty about the world.

It's hard enough to describe the complex phenomena around you to others, so when you do get your message across, it feels rather splendid. However, to do so, you must first make sure your message's receivers have at least built a basic framework around the idea you're referencing. For example, to describe what a molecule is, you must first describe what an atom is. You could then take that thought loop infinitely and say if you want to describe want an atom is, then you must describe what a proton, a neutron, and an electron are.

So we simplify and create basic frameworks of an idea, languages of order that tell us how to communicate ideas most effectively. We say an atom is the smallest observable piece of phenomena, and we can move on and start to fill in the details of the framework on top of that. However, it gets much more complicated when we start using moral and ethical frameworks that come with governing systems and religions to communicate with one another.

The thing is, with so many to choose from, it becomes extremely challenging to decipher the religious philosophies of the modern era. Everyone has a unique set of Thoughtware, of which a different language of order is bound to work for each.

But most of the time, individuals are born into a society with pre-installed order programs, like what defines Christianity, Buddhism, or Hinduism, or the parameters of a functional democracy or a dictatorship. And as we grow up in these societies, we often are coerced into absorbing the religious or political software instead of freely choosing what type of mental governing system might function better for our own individual needs. But integrating psychedelics to achieve a mystical mind might help us grapple with the language of order more suited for our needs.

THOUGHTWARE REBOOT

As Linda Graham, Author of *Bouncing Back,* tells me from her years of experience as a psychotherapist, "From our conditioning every human being has the patterns, they have their beliefs, they have their habits. And very often, we don't even know that we have them, we take them to reality.

And so, it seems what psychedelics can do is help people experience, not even think about, but experience that their mindsets, their filters, their parents, and beliefs are exempt and not who they are. And people can spend many years meditating on retreats, trying to get to that same kind of experience, and psychedelics seem to help people get that in one or two journeys."

In other words, a mystical mind can assist someone by helping them exit mental cycles and formulate more effective ones. It can help an individual reassess their current mindset and re-map their mind. After consuming a psychedelic substance, the mind starts to operate at a different frequency and with it, the emotions it contains, launching the mind into a new state of observatory consciousness with more ease.

However, while in a mindset of observation, it is easy for the ropes of reality to untether, as the psychedelic user becomes prone to venturing past its mental orbit and into the voids of nihilistic insanity. Not being able to return to this mental orbit might be synonymous with an experience labeled as ego-dissolution, in which the previous perceptions of their sense of self must be reconstructed in their entirety—hence the reason some people might describe their psychedelic experience as being *"reborn"*.

We briefly touched on this idea in previous Chapters, the notion of **ego dissolution**, *a type of Thoughtware rebooting protocol*, but I want to fully explore what this concept means and why it's so helpful when formulating more effective languages of order.

In chemistry, a procedure known as recrystallization exists that can describe this spiritual experience. This "is a procedure for purifying an impure compound in a solvent".[118]

For example, given an impure chemical sample crushed into a fine powder, a chemist can re-actualize a chemical 3-D structure, increasing its purity. First, they'll dissolve it in a solution known as a solvent and after allowing the sample time to redevelop as the solvent slowly evaporates off. "The slower the rate of cooling, the larger the crystals are that form." However, done in a bad solvent, the original sample may be destroyed, and a variety of different procedures must be done in order to arrive where the chemist started.

In a similar way, shifting into a mystical frame of mind resonates with this procedure. If done in a safe setting (*the right solvent*), the ego can be dissolved efficiently. Over a prolonged period and with gentle care, the ego can re-precipitate into a refined crystalline version, marked with clarity and sharpness. However, without ample care during the process, the user might re-precipitate as a foggy and dulled crystal, as it still contains trace amounts of impurities.

Thoughtfulness about how our environmental software is interacting in when we try to achieve a mystical mind also becomes apparent. Done in a bad setting, or a bad solvent, the rebirthing processing may be entirely invaluable.[119] So a Medium, a competent individual familiar with this process, may be employed to facilitate the proper use of the psychedelic compound.

Furthering this idea, the emergence of Mediums and ceremonial leaders then also becomes a translucent concept. *They are the chemists of the mind.* They are individuals familiar with the process, supervisors that facilitate the proper use of the psychedelic compound. With the right conditions met, this process, while challenging for the psychedelic consumer, can accomplish profound results in purifying an individual's understanding of the reality they choose to believe in.

But grappling with the idea of using psychedelics to embrace spirituality is a bit too complex for the language of writing. It's like trying to describe the ocean to those who've never set their sights on it. It's impossible to explain its grandiosity with written or vocal language.

So I'll leave you with this one question to answer for yourself in a world driven by metrics and quantifiable systems: **how does one monitor the intangible, the abstract and the bizarre hallucinatory realm of subjectivity.... without first consulting languages of order—forged from uncertainty?**

CHAPTER 10

PSYCHEDELIC CONCLUSIONS

———

Where do you spend most of your time? I don't mean where your physical body is because if we take an abstract point of view, your physical body is only the vehicle you travel in. So let us remove that layer of abstraction and seek a deeper definition when I refer to you.

You are simply an intangible array of neuron impulses, guided by action potentials and external and internal stimuli. Right? Hmm… okay, let's try this… you are your thoughts. The decisions you make, the people you trust or despise, the way you move your body, and the things you do with it. That's you. You are the catalyst of activity, and without you, the physical landscape of the world would have no meaning.

So when I ask, where do you spend your time, I really mean, where are your trains of thought traveling to? Are you heading down the roads of the past, digging up old conversations with your family or friends? Maybe, you're drifting off into a world of fantasy… sandy beaches, bubbly champagne, and warm blankets of summer wind. Whatever the case, we are constantly traveling from location to location in our own minds, and whether these thought trains are indicative of the reality we live in is beside the point.

We are constantly building an interpretative reality of the world we live in because we have been granted the power of imagination. It is our superpower, after all. It allows us to visualize alternate solutions to previous problems, to simulate new environments, and even to predict the next steps we'll take in order to achieve such things. We are constantly fiddling around with the past, present, and future, and so at times, it becomes particularly difficult to answer the question: Where do you spend most of your time? The world we live in is incredibly complex, and our superpower can sometimes behave like a double-edged sword obscuring a purely objective interpretation of the world—a world that stands the test of time.

Throughout this book, we attempted to understand a few prominent mechanisms by which psychedelics can alter this interpretive framework (our Thoughtware) isolating much of our attention to one of its most important layers—**cultural**

software. With many questions still unknown about the exact ways in which psychedelics alter our mental hardware and Thoughtware, as we sailed through humans' relationship with these substances, my hope is that they will start to be taken with more seriousness as research continues to prove promising. On a larger scale, these tools could be wielded to rethink how human civilization operates on a higher level. This is the main idea that I want to instill.

To reinforce this point one last time, we will briefly revisit the areas discussed in this book, starting with the lagging components of modern society and ending with our final conclusions about psychedelics.

* * *

For thousands of years, humans have been pondering foreseeable ways to run better societies, create more tightly knit communities, and promote economic prosperity within their respective cultures. We have been continuously adapting to the harsh stimuli that everyday life brings and have developed one of the most unique cultural software to enable powerful communication within our immediate and now foreign communities.

Whether it be pathological diseases that run rampant across populations or pollutants that sprinkle toxic dust across ecosystems, for every problem that exists, humans have formed some type of imagined order to solve it. The larger the problem, the greater the scope of the imagined order, and that's where we've started to run into problems in the modern era.

Humanity has started setting their sights on exponentially more challenging problems in the twenty-first century and attempted to use ill-suited imagined orders to formulate solutions. We've over incentivized scaling everything to a national and international level (now catalyzed by modern computing) that individuals have started reprogramming their Thoughtware with quantitative commandments of the digital era, embracing a **finite mind** (*observed in Chapter 8*) and forgetting their **language of instinct** (*observed in Chapter 7*).

That's because static and non-adaptive features have begun to burrow in our respective culture as versions of Thoughtware that encourage community-building and cooperation are thrown away. At the end of the day, the **power of problem-solving**, and for that matter, **communication** is only limited by the symbols that transpire with our cultures.

For example, when we visited ancestral cultures, we learned how they used dancing and chanting in conjunction with psychedelics to motivate cooperation and formulate community. However, much of these community-based activities that initially unified the human species for thousands of years are no longer installed in human Thoughtware. These features have largely been cast away in the shadows of economic prosperity.

Instead, we're seeing that (face-to-face) community engagement is at an all-time low, many of the drugs produced by pharmaceutical agencies aimed at treating mental illness have low success rates, and "burn out" is recognized as a legitimate syndrome in the workplace.

While incentivizing economic gain over community has helped launch a plethora of innovative technologies and ideas, it's quite clear that technology has come to bite that hand that fed it with this decision. In turn, it has started placing increasing demands on our attention—disabling us from communicating at a deeper level to form meaningful relationships (*observed in chapter 6*).

This is where we introduce psychedelics into the mix and find out how they could remedy these deep-seated cultural problems embedded within imagined orders.

* * *

To aid us in rethinking these many imagined orders rooted in human societies, we explored three of the most prominent states of mind induced by psychedelic chemicals in this book—the **healing mind**, which helps us relearning the language of instinct and reconnect with both ourselves and others; the **productive mind**, which helps us escape finite games and enter infinite ones; and the **mystical mind**, which helps us recreate how we perceive the very imagined orders that define our cultural software. With these altered states, I aimed to elucidate how influential our current models of the world shape the way we think through describing our cultural software and how psychedelics might offer us an alternative to upgrading the ways in which we think.

Thinking more efficiently is quite simply one of the most valuable things we as a species can actively pursue. More efficient ways of thinking help us engage with each other on deeper levels and unravel insights about the complex contents of reality. If nothing else, understanding how to think better should be at the root of all our decisions. For many of the same reasons that spawned the enlightenment era, we are seeing a rebirth in skepticism about the nature of our rigid bureaucracy that restricts the freedom to explore even our own understandings.

"Since it is the understanding that sets man above all other animals and enables him to use and dominate them, it is certainly worth our while to inquire into it. The understanding is like the eye in this respect: it makes us see and perceive all other things but doesn't look in on itself. To stand back from it and treat it as an object of study requires skill and hard work. Still, whatever difficulties there may be in doing this, **whatever it is that keeps us so much in the dark to ourselves, it will be worthwhile to let as much light as possible in upon our minds, and to learn as much as we can about our own understandings.**"—John Locke[120]

With human understanding forming the foundations for the third wave of the psychedelic revolution, we realized that psychedelics might unlock a version of Thoughtware to help us revise the erroneous systems we have become so attached to. Placing strong attachments on our current cultural software will not solve the issues of the twenty-first century; on the contrary, it might even lead us into a state of madness.

"**There is no madness but that which is in every man**, since it is man who constitutes madness in the attachments he bears for himself and by the **illusions he entertains**... **Self-attachment is the first sign of madness**, but it is because man is attached to himself that he accepts error as truth, lies as reality, violence and ugliness as beauty and justice."—Michel Foucault[121]

Perhaps much of the reason we're afraid of removing our attachments is precisely because we're afraid of unveiling what happens when things do change. Change is like curiosity in that it stimulates growth, innovation, and imagination.

The world around us will not wait, and so we should be careful not to do the same, to not be held back by our own Thoughtware.

And this is no easy task because "It is easy to assume that "nature" is something with a nature—something static. But it's not: at least not in any simple sense. **It's static and dynamic, at the same time.** The environment—the *nature that selects*—itself **transforms.**"

—JORDAN PETERSON[122]

To prepare for the exponential transformations in modern society, we can utilize the unique properties of psychedelics. They can reprogram our Thoughtware to account for the dynamic nature of human civilization. But my goal is not to convince people drugs are the only way to do this, but rather to provide individuals with a framework that helps them decipher why psychedelics can push us into the next step in human evolution.

As we've come to the end of this book, my hopes are we may once again realize how psychedelics can be used to rethink reality—to achieve a Mind Leap.

ACKNOWLEDGEMENTS

Throughout the arduous journey of writing a book about the most controversial class of drugs, I was fortunate to have a loving family and supportive group of friends that always let me read them my crazy ideas. Special thanks to my friends Austin, Mike and Will for listening to me read parts of my book hours on end.

Thank you to all those who took time out of their day to let me interview them and help me charge through the realms of psychedelic and psychiatric exploration. Without their guidance and intellectual wisdom regarding this complex subject matter, this book would never have been possible. Here are the individuals that I spoke with that sharpened this book's insights:

Brad Burge (Director of Strategic Communication for MAPS)

Ben Sessa (Medical Doctor for Mandala Therapy Limited and Author of The Psychedelic Renaissance)

Linda Graham (Author and Psychotherapist)

David Nichols (Founder of Heffter Research Institute for Psychedelic Studies)

Michael Winkelman (Professor at Arizona State University and Author of Supernatural as Natural)

Sirley Bonham (Theoretical Physics Researcher at The University of Texas at Austin)

Stan Franklin (Professor at the University of Memphis and Author of Artificial Minds)

Marina Bystritsky (Clinical Psychologist)

A MASSIVE Thank you to every at New Degree Press, specifically, **Professor Eric Koester** and **Brian Bies,** who had to put up with me constantly trying to delay deadlines just to spend an extra day rewriting one sentence, and **Stephanie Mckibben, Stephanie Gillet,** and **Cynthia Tucker,** (*my editors*) who had the unfortunate duty of turning my mess of thoughts into coherent English. I can't thank them enough for helping me transform my ideas into a what is now a fully formed book!

Thank you to those who supported Mind Leap's pre-order campaign and helped me make this book come to life with their generous donations and support:

Alexis Huynh
Allison Huynh
Amanda Cramer
Ana Jordan
Andrew Aman
Andrew Ellinor
Andrew Ginac
Arthur Ardelea
Austin Ward
Bernard Newman
Beth Josephs
Brian Ferry
Caleb Hollifield
Charles Hibler
Chris Protass
Connor Dilgren
Dana Germer
Denise DeMartino
Ed Dunn
Eric Kasper
Eric Koester
Frank Ginac
Georgia Spencer

Gian Micah Zani
Grayce Parker
Gregory Aman
Harlin Teague
Hunter Hershey
James Cramer
James Dial
James Hamel
James Robertson
Jay Sexton
Jeff Friedberg
Jennifer Lavoie
Jeremy DiGiovanni
JJ Meador
John Cramer
Jonathan Friedberg
Jorge Luis Barron
Joseph Schroer
Josh Block
Josh Syre
Kimberly Metzger
Kimberly Miller
Kristen Gentry

Kyle Lottinville

Lea Anderson

Lee Carnes

Linda Graham

Lorin Cramer

MacKenzie Darilek

Mackenzie Finklea

Martin Pham

Marwan Madi

Mary Jo Dono

Mason Foster

Melanie Aman

Micaela Roybal

Mira Roosth

Naili Salehuddin

Natalie Stephens

Nicholas C Turner

Nicholas Minutaglio

Nicholas Robert Tyler

Nicole Hershey

Nicole Otramba

Nithin Kakulavaram

Patrick Lyons

Paul Yeric

Peter D'Andrea

Quinlan S. Sweeney

Raj Sharan

Raymond Collins

Reilly Higgs

Richard Ahn

Rishan Chamdal

Robert Woodruff

Roshan Chandrashekar

Sagar Segal

Samyukta Singh

Sarah Walsh Roberts

Sean MacIntyre

Seth Aldrich

Shan Ali

Shante-Isabel Atillo

Shelley Parker

Sierra Latshaw

Tammy Caciola

Tara Heavner

Tracy Aman

Trevor Hershey

Troy Pawlak

Vinit Nagaich

William Henry Robert

Zhenyu Liu

CITATIONS

INTRODUCTION

1. Solon, Olivia. "Elon Musk Says Humans Must Become Cyborgs to Stay Relevant. Is He Right?" The Guardian. Guardian News and Media, February 15, 2017. https://www.theguardian.com/technology/2017/feb/15/elon-musk-cyborgs-robots-artificial-intelligence-is-he-right.

2. CBC News: The National. "Yuval Harari warns about the potential of AI." *Youtube* video, 2:13. September 34, 2018. https://www.youtube.com/watch?v=HGTGoRrzItA&t=137s

3. Popham, James W. "Why Standardized Tests Don't Measure Educational Quality." Why Standardized Tests Don't Measure Educational Quality - Educational Leadership. ASCD, 1999. http://www.ascd.org/publications/educational-leadership/mar99/vol56/num06/Why-Standardized-Tests-Don't-Measure-Educational-Quality.aspx.

4. "Overview: Learning to Realize Education's Promise." *World Development Report 2018: Learning to Realize Educations Promise*, 2017, 1–35. https://doi.org/10.1596/978-1- 4648-1096-1_ov.

5. TED. "How to escape education's death valley | Sir Ken Robinson." *Youtube* video, 9:31. May 10, 2013. https://www.youtube.com/watch?v=wX78iKhInsc&t=472s

6. Schwartz, Lisa M., and Steven Woloshin. "Medical Marketing in the United States, 1997-2016." *Jama* 321, no. 1 (January 2019): 80. https://doi.org/10.1001/jama.2018.19320.

7. "7 Staggering Statistics About America's Opioid Epidemic." American Physical Therapy Association. ChoosePT, September 30, 2019. https://www.choosept.com/resources/detail/7-staggering-statistics-about-america-s-opioid-epi.

8. "ANNUAL U.S. Deaths from Psychedelics Compared to Other Causes by Gustavo Serrano." Infogram. infogram. Accessed October 10, 2019. https://infogram.com/annual-us-deaths-from-psychedelics-compared-to-other-causes-1gvew2ve5v5nmnj.

9. "LSD Fact Sheet." Drug Policy Alliance, January 5, 2017. http://www.drugpolicy.org/resource/lsd-fact-sheet.

10. Sahakian, Barbara. "'Microdosing' LSD Is Not Just a Silicon Valley Trend – It Is Spreading to Other Workplaces." The Independent. Independent Digital News and Media, August 22, 2018. https://www.independent.co.uk/voices/lsd-microdosing-california-silicon-valley-california-drugs-young-professionals-a8259001.html.

11. Isaacson, Walter, and Steve Jobs. *Steve Jobs.* London: Abacus, 2015. 52-53

CHAPTER 1

12. *Limitless*, n.d.

13. TED-Ed. "How we conquered the deadly smallpox virus - Simona Zompi." *Youtube* video, October 28, 2013. https://www.youtube.com/watch?v=yqUFy-t4MlQ

14. "FastStats - Immunization." Centers for Disease Control and Prevention. Centers for Disease Control and Prevention, 2017. https://www.cdc.gov/nchs/fastats/immunize.htm.

15. "Vaccine Preventable Adult Diseases | CDC." Centers for Disease Control and Prevention. Centers for Disease Control and Prevention. Accessed October 10, 2019. https://www.cdc.gov/vaccines/adults/vpd.html.

16. "FastStats - Immunization." Centers for Disease Control and Prevention. Centers for Disease Control and Prevention, 2017. https://www.cdc.gov/nchs/fastats/immunize.htm.

17. "Generic Antidepressants Can Save Consumers $1,200 a Year." Advocacy. Advocacy, February 10, 2005. https://advocacy.consumerreports.org/press_release/generic-antidepressants-can-save-consumers-1200-a-year/.

18. Boseley, Sarah. "The Drugs Do Work: Antidepressants Are Effective, Study Shows." The Guardian. Guardian News and Media, February 21, 2018. https://www.theguardian.com/science/2018/feb/21/the-drugs-do-work-antidepressants-are-effective-study-shows.

19. Thiel, Edwin Van. "What Are the Big Five Personality Test Traits? - Learn All about the Theory." 123test, September 10, 2018. https://www.123test.com/big-five-personality-theory/.

20. Erritzoe, D., L. Roseman, M. M. Nour, K. MacLean, M. Kaelen, D. J. Nutt, and R. L. Carhart-Harris. "Effects of Psilocybin Therapy on Personality Structure." Wiley Online Library. John Wiley & Sons, Ltd (10.1111), June 19, 2018. https://onlinelibrary.wiley.com/doi/full/10.1111/acps.12904.

21. Srivastava, Sanjay, Oliver P John, Samuel D Gosling, and Jeff Potter. "Development of Personality in Early and Middle Adulthood: Set like Plaster or Persistent Change?" Journal of personality and social psychology. U.S. National Library of Medicine, May 2003. https://www.ncbi.nlm.nih.gov/pubmed/12757147.

22. Timeline – World History Documentaries. "The Mystery Of The Pyramids: Egypt Detectives (Ancient Egypt Documentary) | Timeline." *Youtube* video, 5:40. November 30, 2017. https://www.youtube.com/watch?v=yqUFy-t4MlQ

23. Twenge, Jean M., A. Bell Cooper, Thomas E. Joiner, Mary E. Duffy, and Sarah G. Binau. "Age, Period, and Cohort Trends in Mood Disorder Indicators and Suicide-Related Outcomes in a Nationally Representative Dataset, 2005–2017." *Journal of Abnormal Psychology* 128, no. 3 (2019): 185–99. https://doi.org/10.1037/abn0000410.

24. Cal, Newport. *Digital Minimalism*. Random House USA, 2019.

25. Schawbel, Dan. "Brene Brown: How Vulnerability Can Make Our Lives Better." Forbes. Forbes Magazine, April 21, 2013. https://www.forbes.com/sites/danschawbel/2013/04/21/brene-brown-how-vulnerability-can-make-our-lives-better/#79ddaff536c7.

26. "Depression Is on the Rise in the U.S., Especially Among Young Teens." Search the website. Columbia University, October 30, 2017. https://www.mailman.columbia.edu/public-health-now/news/depression-rise-us-especially-among-young-teens.

27. Morin-Major, Julie Katia, Marie-France Marin, Nadia Durand, Nathalie Wan, Robert-Paul Juster, and Sonia J Lupien. "Facebook Behaviors Associated with Diurnal Cortisol in Adolescents: Is Befriending Stressful?" Psychoneuroendocrinology. U.S. National Library of Medicine, January 2016. https://www.ncbi.nlm.nih.gov/pubmed/26519778.

28. "The 'Loneliness Epidemic.'" Health Resources & Services Administration, January 10, 2019. https://www.hrsa.gov/enews/past-issues/2019/january-17/loneliness-epidemic.

29. Davey, Graham C.L. "Social Media, Loneliness, and Anxiety in Young People." Psychology Today. Sussex Publishers, December 15, 2016. https://www.psychologytoday.com/us/blog/why-we-worry/201612/social-media-loneliness-and-anxiety-in-young-people.

CHAPTER 2

30. Times, Carl Velasco Tech. "Dopamine Is The Reason Why Humans Are So Unique From Other Animals." Tech Times. TechScienceHealthCulture Features Buzz, November 25, 2017. https://www.techtimes.com/articles/216122/20171124/dopamine-is-the-reason-why-humans-are-so-unique-from-other-animals.htm.

31. Volkow, N D, G-J Wang, J Logan, D Alexoff, J S Fowler, P K Thanos, C Wong, V Casado, S Ferre, and D Tomasi. "Caffeine Increases Striatal Dopamine D2/D3 Receptor Availability in the Human Brain." Translational psychiatry. Nature Publishing Group, April 14, 2015. https://www.ncbi.nlm.nih.gov/pmc/articles/PMC4462609/.

32. Guy, Peter. "Why Bankers and Cocaine Are Best of Friends." South China Morning Post, July 20, 2018. https://www.scmp.com/business/article/2041361/why-bankers-and-cocaine-are-best-of-friends.

33. Sullivan, Roger J, Edward H Hagen, and Peter Hammerstein. "Revealing the Paradox of Drug Reward in Human Evolution." Proceedings. Biological sciences. The Royal Society, June 7, 2008. https://www.ncbi.nlm.nih.gov/pmc/articles/PMC2367444/.

34. Brusco, Robert. "Tripping through Time: The Fascinating History of the Magic Mushroom." Ancient Origins. Ancient Origins, February 1, 2017. https://www.ancient-origins.net/history-ancient-traditions/tripping-through-time-fascinating-history-magic-mushroom-007474.

35. National Institute on Drug Abuse. "How Do Hallucinogens (LSD, Psilocybin, Peyote, DMT, and Ayahuasca) Affect the Brain and Body?" NIDA. National Institute on Drug Abuse, February 2015. https://www.drugabuse.gov/publications/hallucinogens-dissociative-drugs/how-do-hallucinogens-lsd-psilocybin-peyote-dmt-ayahuasca-affect-brain-body.

36. John-Smith, Paul St, Daniel Mcqueen, Lindsey Edwards, and Fabrizio Schifano. "Classical and Novel Psychoactive Substances: Rethinking Drug Misuse from an Evolutionary Psychiatric Perspective." *Human Psychopharmacology: Clinical and Experimental* 28, no. 4 (July 23, 2013): 394–401. https://doi.org/10.1002/hup.2303.

37. McCarthy, Matt. *Superbugs: The Race to Stop an Epidemic*. Penguin Publishing Group, 2019.

38. Kawai, Nobuyuki, and Hongshen He. "Breaking Snake Camouflage: Humans Detect Snakes More Accurately than Other Animals under Less Discernible Visual Conditions." PLOS ONE. Public Library of Science, October 26, 2016. https://journals.plos.org/plosone/article?id=10.1371/journal.pone.0164342.

39. Vollenweider, F X. "Brain Mechanisms of Hallucinogens and Entactogens." Dialogues inclinical neuroscience. Les Laboratoires Servier, December 2001. https://www.ncbi.nlm.nih.gov/pmc/articles/PMC3181663/.

40. "Researchers Report Vision-Based Neurotransmitter Events for the First Time." Medical Xpress - medical research advances and health news. Medical Xpress, November 27, 2018. https://medicalxpress.com/news/2018-11-vision-based-neurotransmitter- events.html.

CHAPTER 3

41. "Popular Culture and Mass Media in the 1950s." Khan Academy. Khan Academy. Accessed October 22, 2019. https://www.khanacademy.org/humanities/us- history/postwarera/1950s-america/a/popular-culture-and-mass-media-cnx.

42. Madrigal, Alexis C. "When Did TV Watching Peak?" Bunk History, May 30, 2018. https://www.bunkhistory.org/resources/2630?related=1420&relationship_name=ANOTHER ANGLE.

43. Hanke, Stacey. "How Social Media Affects Our Ability to Communicate." How Social Media Affects Our Ability to Communicate.

Thrive Global, September 13, 2018. https://thriveglobal.com/stories/
how-social-media-affects-our-ability-to-communicate/.

44. Darwin, Charles, and Jim Endersby. *On the Origin of Species*. Cambridge:
Cambridge University Press, 2009.

45. BUSS, DAVID. *EVOLUTIONARY PSYCHOLOGY the New Science of the
Mind*. Place of publication not identified: ROUTLEDGE, 2019.

46. WINKELMAN, MICHAEL. *SUPERNATURAL AS NATURAL: a Biocultural
Approach to Religion*. Place of publication not identified: ROUTLEDGE, 2017.

47. Vox. "The surprising pattern behind color names around the
world". *Youtube* video. May 16, 2017. https://www.youtube.com/
watch?v=gMqZR3pqMjg&t=194s

48. Tom Bilyeu. "Brain Surgeon's Advice On How To Stop Negative Behaviors
And Strengthen Your Mind." *Youtube* video, 4:12. July 11, 2019. https://www.
youtube.com/watch?v=x29hY6_8bDg

49. Ward, Peter. "Are Human Genes Changing As Fast As Culture
and Technology?" Are Human Genes Changing As Fast As Culture
and Technology? Literary Hub, April 2, 2019. https://lithub.com/
are-human-genes-changing-as-fast-as-culture-and-technology/.

50. Shepherd, Christian. "Chinese Scientist Who Gene-Edited Babies Fired
by University." Edited by Nick Macfie and Hugh Lawson. Reuters. Thomson
Reuters, January 21, 2019. https://www.reuters.com/article/us-china-health-
babies/chinese-scientist-who-gene-edited-babies-fired-by-university-
idUSKCN1PF0RA.

51. Project, Borgen. "Modern Countries That Still Have Slavery." The Borgen
Project. Borgen Project https://borgenproject.org/wp-content/uploads/The_
Borgen_Project_Logo_small.jpg, September 26, 2018. https://borgenproject.
org/countries-that-still-have-slavery/.

52. Wei, Katherine. "How Many People Do You Need to Change the
Culture?" Sierra Club, June 9, 2018. https://www.sierraclub.org/sierra/
how-change-peoples-minds-25-percent-tipping-point.

53. Montolíu, Rubén Moreno. "Agriculture and Greenhouse Gas Emissions."
American Farm Bureau Federation - The Voice of Agriculture, March 5, 2019.
https://www.fb.org/market-intel/agriculture-and-greenhouse-gas-emissions.

54. Steinfeld, Henning. *Livestocks Long Shadow: Environmental Issues and Options*. Rom: Food and Agriculture Organization of the United Nations, 2006.

55. McNeill, William Hardy. *A World History*. New York: Oxford University Press, 1999.

56. Pobiner, Briana. "Evidence for Meat-Eating by Early Humans." Nature News. Nature Publishing Group, 2013. https://www.nature.com/scitable/knowledge/library/evidence-for-meat-eating-by-early-humans-103874273/.

57. Hacker, J. David. "Recounting the Dead." The New York Times. The New York Times, September 21, 2011. https://opinionator.blogs.nytimes.com/2011/09/20/recounting-the-dead/.

CHAPTER 4

58. Pollan, Michael. *How to Change Your Mind: What the New Science of Psychedelics Teaches Us about Consciousness, Dying, Addiction, Depression, and Transcendence*. New York: Penguin Press, 2019.

59. 2010, The Pharmaceutical Journal17 DEC. "The Animal World Has Its Junkies Too." Pharmaceutical Journal, December 17, 2010. https://www.pharmaceutical-journal.com/opinion/comment/the-animal-world-has-its-junkies-too/11052360.article?firstPass=false.

60. Witt, Peter N. "Drugs Alter Web-Building of Spiders: A Review and Evaluation." *Behavioral Science* 16, no. 1 (1971): 98–113. https://doi.org/10.1002/bs.3830160109.

61. Lewis-Williams, J. D., T. A. Dowson, Paul G. Bahn, Robert G. Bednarik, John Clegg, Mario Consens, Whitney Davis, et al. "The Signs of All Times: Entoptic Phenomena in Upper Palaeolithic Art [and Comments and Reply]." *Current Anthropology* 29, no. 2 (1988): 201–45. https://doi.org/10.1086/203629.

62. Mark, Joshua J. "Cuneiform." Ancient History Encyclopedia. Ancient History Encyclopedia, October 21, 2019. https://www.ancient.eu/cuneiform/.

63. Reichel-Dolmatoff, Gerardo. *Amazonian Cosmos*. Place of publication not identified, 1971.

64. Bressloff, Paul C., Jack D. Cowan, Martin Golubitsky, Peter J. Thomas, and Matthew C. Wiener. "What Geometric Visual Hallucinations Tell Us about the Visual Cortex." *Neural Computation* 14, no. 3 (2002): 473–91. https://doi.org/10.1162/089976602317250861.

65. "THE OLDEST REPRESENTATIONS OF HALLUCINOGENIC MUSHROOMS IN THE WORLD (SAHARA DESERT, 9000 – 7000 B.P.)." Artepreistoricacom RSS. Accessed October 23, 2019. http://www.artepreistorica. com/2009/12/the-oldest-representations-of-hallucinogenic-mushrooms-in-the-world-sahara-desert-9000---7000-b-p/.

66. MAPS. "Paul Stamets: Psilocybin Mushrooms & The Mycology of Consciousness." *Youtube* video, 13:30. May 11, 2017. https://www.youtube.com/watch?v=vFWxWqoFvoU&t=1468s

CHAPTER 5

67. Mark, Joshua J. "War in Ancient Times." Ancient History Encyclopedia. Ancient History Encyclopedia, October 20, 2019. https://www.ancient.eu/war/.

68. GILES, HERBERT ALLEN. *RELIGIONS OF ANCIENT CHINA.* S.l.: EARNSHAW BOOKS LIMITED, 2020.

69. Levin, Jeff. "Religion and Mental Health: Theory and Research." *International Journal of Applied Psychoanalytic Studies,* 2010. https://doi. org/10.1002/aps.240.

70. Koenig, Harold George. *The Healing Power of Faith: Science Explores Medicines Last Frontier.* London: Simon & Schuster, 2002.

71. Burn-Callander, Rebecca. "The History of Money: from Barter to Bitcoin." The Telegraph. Telegraph Media Group, October 20, 2014. https://www. telegraph.co.uk/finance/businessclub/money/11174013/The-history-of-money-from-barter-to-bitcoin.html.

72. Wing, Nick, and Carolyn Gregoire. "The More We Learn About Psychedelic Mushrooms, The More Fascinating They Become." HuffPost. HuffPost, December 7, 2017. https://www.huffpost.com/entry/psychedelic-mushrooms-facts_n_6083436.

73. Gossop, Michael. *Living with Drugs.* London: Temple Smith, 1982.

74. Crocq, Marc-Antoine. "Historical and Cultural Aspects of Man's Relationship with Addictive Drugs." Dialogues in clinical neuroscience. Les Laboratoires Servier, 2007. https://www.ncbi.nlm.nih.gov/pmc/articles/PMC3202501/.

75. "Make Love Not War." The Hippie Movement, April 30, 2015. https://blogs. stockton.edu/hippiemovement/make-love-not-war/.

76. Harris, Mark. "The Flowering of the Hippies." The Atlantic. Atlantic Media Company, April 12, 2018. https://www.theatlantic.com/magazine/archive/1967/09/the-flowering-of-the-hippies/306619/.

77. Bedard, Paul. "Jail Survey: 7 in 10 Felons Register as Democrats." Washington Examiner, January 1, 2014. https://www.washingtonexaminer.com/jail-survey-7-in-10-felons-register-as-democrats.

78. Saad, Lydia. "In U.S., 38% Have Tried Marijuana, Little Changed Since '80s." Gallup.com. Gallup, April 23, 2019. https://news.gallup.com/poll/163835/tried-marijuana-little-changed-80s.aspx.

79. Newport, Frank. "Democrats Racially Diverse; Republicans Mostly White." Gallup.com. Gallup, June 24, 2018. https://news.gallup.com/poll/160373/democrats-racially-diverse-republicans-mostly-white.aspx.

80. DEA Public Affairs. "LSD: The Drug." DEA - Publications - LSD in the US - The Drug. Accessed October 23, 2019. http://www.druglibrary.net/schaffer/dea/pubs/lsd/LSD-4.htm.

81. "A Brief History of the Drug War." Drug Policy Alliance. Accessed October 23, 2019. http://www.drugpolicy.org/issues/brief-history-drug-war.

82. TEDx Talks. "Psychedelics: Past, present and future | Mark Haden | TEDxEastVan." *Youtube* video, 0:40. November 21, 2017. https://www.youtube.com/watch?v=JI1dwVsPw2E

CHAPTER 6

82. Candid. "Johns Hopkins Receives $17 Million for Research on Pyschedelics." Philanthropy News Digest (PND), September 6, 2019. https://philanthropynewsdigest.org/news/johns-hopkins-receives-17-million-for-research-on-pyschedelics#targetText=Johns Hopkins University has announced,for Psychedelic and Consciousness Research.

83. Grof, Stanislav. *LSD Psychotherapy*. Sarasota, FL: Multidisciplinary Association for Psychedelic Studies, 2001.

84. "The NCES Fast Facts Tool Provides Quick Answers to Many Education Questions (National Center for Education Statistics)." National Center for Education Statistics (NCES) Home Page, a part of the U.S. Department of Education. Accessed October 23, 2019. https://nces.ed.gov/fastfacts/display.asp?id=40.

85. Greene, Tim. "10 Of the World's Fastest Supercomputers." Network World. IDG News Service, June 17, 2019. https://www.networkworld.com/article/3236875/embargo-10-of-the-worlds-fastest-supercomputers.html#slide11.

86. "Physiology." Encyclopædia Britannica. Encyclopædia Britannica, inc. Accessed October 23, 2019. https://www.britannica.com/science/information-theory/Physiology.

87. Winkelman, Michael. "Shamanism as a Biogenetic Structural Paradigm for Humans' Evolved Social Psychology." *Psychology of Religion and Spirituality 7*, no. 4 (2015): 267–77. https://doi.org/10.1037/rel0000034.

88. Belludi, Nagesh. "Albert Mehrabian's 7-38-55 Rule of Personal Communication." Right Attitudes, October 27, 2017. https://www.rightattitudes.com/2008/10/04/7-38-55-rule-personal-communication/.

89. Ellens, J. Harold. *Seeking the Sacred with Psychoactive Substances: Chemical Paths to Spirituality and to God.* Santa Barbara (Calif.): Praeger, 2014.

90. Satariano, Adam. "Facebook Identifies Russia-Linked Misinformation Campaign." The New York Times. The New York Times, January 17, 2019. https://www.nytimes.com/2019/01/17/business/facebook-misinformation-russia.html.

91. Korteling, Johan E, Anne-Marie Brouwer, and Alexander Toet. "A Neural Network Framework for Cognitive Bias." Frontiers in psychology. Frontiers Media S.A., September 3, 2018. https://www.ncbi.nlm.nih.gov/pmc/articles/PMC6129743/.

92. Krögeri, Ronald H.H, Eric Warranti, and Anna Gislen. "Superior Underwater Vision in a Human Population of Sea Gypsies." Current Biology. Cell Press, May 15, 2003. https://www.sciencedirect.com/science/article/pii/S0960982203002902.

93. Komninos, Andreas. "The Concept of the 'Triune Brain.'" The Interaction Design Foundation. Accessed October 23, 2019. https://www.interaction-design.org/literature/article/the-concept-of-the-triune-brain.

94. Sample, Ian. "LSD's Impact on the Brain Revealed in Groundbreaking Images." The Guardian. Guardian News and Media, April 11, 2016. https://www.theguardian.com/science/2016/apr/11/lsd-impact-brain-revealed-groundbreaking-images.

95. Winkelman, Michael J. "The Mechanisms of Psychedelic Visionary Experiences: Hypotheses from Evolutionary Psychology." Frontiers in neuroscience. Frontiers Media S.A., September 28, 2017. https://www.ncbi.nlm. nih.gov/pmc/articles/PMC5625021/#B153.

96. Millière, Raphaël, Robin L Carhart-Harris, Leor Roseman, Fynn-Mathis Trautwein, and Aviva Berkovich-Ohana. "Psychedelics, Meditation, and Self-Consciousness." Frontiers in psychology. Frontiers Media S.A., September 4, 2018. https://www.ncbi.nlm.nih.gov/pmc/articles/PMC6137697/.

97. Garrison, Kathleen A, Thomas A Zeffiro, Dustin Scheinost, R Todd Constable, and Judson A Brewer. "Meditation Leads to Reduced Default Mode Network Activity beyond an Active Task." Cognitive, affective & behavioral neuroscience. U.S. National Library of Medicine, September 2015. https://www. ncbi.nlm.nih.gov/pmc/articles/PMC4529365/.

98. Ly, Calvin, Alexandra C Greb, Lindsay P Cameron, Jonathan M Wong, Eden V Barragan, Paige C Wilson, Kyle F Burbach, et al. "Psychedelics Promote Structural and Functional Neural Plasticity." Cell reports. U.S. National Library of Medicine, June 12, 2018. https://www.ncbi.nlm.nih.gov/pmc/articles/PMC6082376/.

99. Nichols, David E. "Psychedelics." Pharmacological reviews. The American Society for Pharmacology and Experimental Therapeutics, April 2016. https:// www.ncbi.nlm.nih.gov/pmc/articles/PMC4813425/.

CHAPTER 7

100. Seth, Michael J. "South Korea's Economic Development, 1948–1996." Oxford Research Encyclopedia of Asian History, July 17, 2019. https:// oxfordre.com/asianhistory/view/10.1093/acrefore/9780190277727.001.0001/ acrefore-9780190277727-e-271.

101. "Our World in Data." Our World in Data. Accessed October 23, 2019. https://ourworldindata.org/.

102. Koo, Soo Kyung. "Depression Status in Korea." Osong public health and research perspectives. Korea Centers for Disease Control and Prevention, August 2018. https://www.ncbi.nlm.nih.gov/pmc/articles/PMC6110326/.

103. David Crossman. "Simon Sinek on Millennials in the Workplace." Youtube video, 5:40. October 19, 2016. https://www.youtube.com/ watch?v=hERoQp6QJNU

104. Gunderson, Adam, Doug Bonderud, Kelly McSweeney, and Rick Robinson. "The Intersection of Technology, Innovation & Creativity." Now. Powered by Northrop Grumman. Accessed October 23, 2019. https://now.northropgrumman.com/ this-is-your-brain-on-instagram-effects-of-social-media-on-the-brain/.

105. Hartley, Stephen, Trevor, Eric Jones, Trevor Haynes, Youcef Chakib Hacene, George, Mona Arora, et al. "Dopamine, Smartphones & You: A Battle for Your Time." Science in the News, February 27, 2019. http://sitn.hms.harvard. edu/flash/2018/dopamine-smartphones-battle-time/.

106. Rizzolatti1, Giacomo, and Laila Craighero21Dipartimento di Neuroscienze. "THE MIRROR-NEURON SYSTEM." Annual Reviews. Accessed October 23, 2019. https://www.annualreviews.org/doi/10.1146/annurev.neuro.27.070203.144230.

107. Komninos, Andreas. "Our Three Brains - The Emotional Brain." The Interaction Design Foundation. Accessed October 23, 2019. https://www. interaction-design.org/literature/article/our-three-brains-the-emotional-brain.

108. Winkelman, Michael. "Shamanic Cosmology as an Evolutionary Neurocognitive Epistemology." *International Journal of Transpersonal Studies* 32, no. 1 (January 2013): 79–99. https://doi.org/10.24972/ijts.2013.32.1.79.

109. "MDMA-Assisted Psychotherapy." MAPS. Accessed October 23, 2019. https://maps.org/research/mdma.

110. Morris, Shaun. "'Magic Mushrooms' Can Help Smokers Break the Habit." Johns Hopkins Medicine, September 16, 2014. https://www.hopkinsmedicine. org/news/stories/mushrooms_quit_smoking.html.

CHAPTER 8

111. Newcomb, Alyssa. "The Biggest Business Bankruptcies of 2018." NBCNews. com. NBCUniversal News Group, December 28, 2018. https://www.nbcnews. com/business/business-news/biggest-business-bankruptcies-2018-n952251.

112. Nordstrom, David Sturt and Todd. "10 Shocking Workplace Stats You Need To Know." Forbes. Forbes Magazine, March 8, 2018. https://www.forbes. com/sites/davidsturt/2018/03/08/10-shocking-workplace-stats-you-need-to-know/#7848e6a2f3af.

113. Veylan, Bhavani. The Truth About Millennial Turnover. Accessed October 23, 2019. https://www.recruiting.com/blog/ the-truth-about-millennial-turnover/.

114. Cassella, Carly. "'Burn-Out' Is Now a Legitimate Syndrome According to The WHO. Here Are The Symptoms." ScienceAlert. Accessed October 23, 2019. https://www.sciencealert.com/burn-out-is-now-officially-recognised-as-a-legitimate-syndrome-by-the-world-health-organisation.

115. Adkins, Amy. "Millennials: The Job-Hopping Generation." Gallup.com. Gallup, July 5, 2018. https://www.gallup.com/workplace/231587/millennials-job-hopping-generation.aspx.

116. Sample, Ian. "LSD's Impact on the Brain Revealed in Groundbreaking Images." The Guardian. Guardian News and Media, April 11, 2016. https://www.theguardian.com/science/2016/apr/11/lsd-impact-brain-revealed-groundbreaking-images.

117. Polito, Vince, and Richard J. Stevenson. "A Systematic Study of Microdosing Psychedelics." PLOS ONE. Public Library of Science. Accessed October 23, 2019. https://journals.plos.org/plosone/article?id=10.1371/journal.pone.0211023.

CHAPTER 9

118. Libretexts. "Recrystallization." Chemistry LibreTexts. Libretexts, June 5, 2019. https://chem.libretexts.org/Bookshelves/Physical_and_Theoretical_Chemistry_Textbook_Maps/Supplemental_Modules_(Physical_and_Theoretical_Chemistry)/Physical_Properties_of_Matter/Solutions_and_Mixtures/Case_Studies/RECRYSTALLIZATION.

119. Nolan, James. "Competitive Psychedelic Users Are Chasing 'Ego Death' and Losing Their Sense of Self." Vice, November 14, 2018. https://www.vice.com/en_us/article/j5zqwp/competitive-psychedelic-users-are-chasing-ego-death-and-losing-their-sense-of-self.

CHAPTER 10

120. Locke, John, and P. H. Nidditch. *An Essay Concerning Human Understanding.* Oxford: Clarendon Press, 2011.

121. Foucault, Michel. *Madness and Civilization.* New York: London, 2001.

122. Peterson, Jordan B, Norman Doidge, and Ethan Van Sciver. *12 Rules for Life: an Antidote to Chaos.* London: Penguin Books, 2019.

www.ingramcontent.com/pod-product-compliance
Lightning Source LLC
Chambersburg PA
CBHW071520180526
45171CB00002B/325